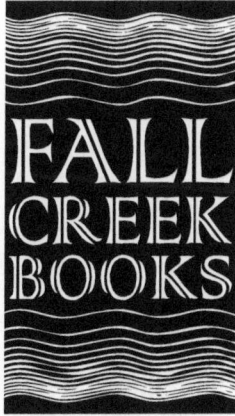

ABOUT FALL CREEK BOOKS

Fall Creek Books is an imprint of Cornell University Press dedicated to making available again classic books that document the history, culture, natural history, and folkways of New York State. Presented in new paperback editions that faithfully reproduce the contents of the original editions, Fall Creek Books titles will appeal to all readers interested in New York and the state's rich past. Some of the books published under this imprint reflect the sensibilities and attitudes of an earlier era; these views do not necessarily reflect those of Cornell University Press.

For a complete listing of titles published under the Fall Creek Books imprint, please visit: cornellpress.cornell.edu.

THE BUILDING OF CITIES

Development and Conflict

HARVEY H. KAISER

Fall Creek Books
AN IMPRINT OF
CORNELL UNIVERSITY PRESS
ITHACA AND LONDON

First published in 1978 by Cornell University Press
First printing, Fall Creek Books, 2013

Library of Congress Cataloging in Publication Data
(For library cataloging purposes only)

Kaiser, Harvey H   1936–
  The building of cities.
  Includes bibliographical references and index.
  ISBN 978-0-8014-7903-8 (paper: alk. paper)
    1. New towns—United States—Case studies.   2. Community development—United States—Case studies.   3. City planning—United States—Case Studies.   4. New towns—New York (State)—Case studies.   5. Community development—New York (State)—Case studies.   6. City planning—New York (State)—Case studies.   I. Title.
HT167.K29   1978   301.36′3′0973   77-3118

Cornell University Press strives to use environmentally responsible suppliers and materials to the fullest extent possible in the publishing of its books. Such materials include vegetable-based, low-VOC inks and acid-free papers that are recycled, totally chlorine-free, or partly composed of nonwood fibers. For further information, visit our website at www.cornellpress.cornell.edu.

Preface

This book is about the process of urban development and what occurs in a community as residents react to proposed changes in the local setting; it is about the individuals and groups that participate in the process of building cities; it also tells us much about the building of new towns. We need to know who is building our cities and who built the ones we have. Do landowners, developers, public officials, or governments control the where, when, and how of development?

I have sought answers to these questions by looking closely at the city-building process from the time when a proposal is first conceived to the early stages of construction. I have long been puzzled about the events that occur in a community when a master plan, an urban development scheme, a request for a zoning change, or some other form of community development is proposed. Some communities openly accept suggestions for change. In others, intensive conflict is generated, and reaching agreement can be time consuming and expensive to the parties involved. The different reactions can have ineradicable effects in the community.

Why do communities in the same region react differently to similar proposals designed to meet local needs? And what factors influence the emergence of controversy over proposals for urban development? An exciting type of development that has caught national attention provides the opportunity to look closely at what happens to the property owners and residents located at the site of a proposed development. In the Housing and Urban Development Act of 1970 (and particularly Title VII of the Act) the United States Congress provided support for "New Communities"—also known as "New Towns." Three communities in upstate New York responded to Title VII and applied for federal aid under the Act. One of the proposals discussed here was sponsored by a public agency (New York State Urban Development Corporation), the other two by private developers. Lysander (later renamed Radisson) is in the Syracuse area; in the Rochester area are Gananda and Riverton. Source documents for the three communities are similar, were prepared in the same time period, and are comparable. We will examine these three proposals to understand the situations that evolve during the early stages of development.

My approach is intended to provide information on how *any* type of development evolves and how community reaction occurs and what forms it may take. The chapters that follow describe what occurs in a community during the presentation of a proposal, how parties to the proposal interact with each other, and how the "climate" of a community influences all parties' actions. This approach will allow students, elected officials, appointed officials, and professionals engaged in development or environmental design to benefit from past experiences.

Several factors central to understanding the entire process of urban development include understanding the leadership of groups involved, the way a proposal is presented to a community, and the ways in which the community is affected by the proposal. The study uncovered five concerns of local residents, expressed as: (1) the effect of the proposal on the present way of life; (2) the economic impact on the residents; (3) the economic impact on the community; (4) the effect of the proposal on the existing level and quality of community services; and (5) the structure of the existing government and its relationship to proposed development.

The investigation reported here is a relatively unprecedented endeavor. Not only is there a lack of earlier work in the environmental design literature but, similarly, little work has been done in the social sciences on the processes involved at the inception of a land-development proposal. The decision to undertake a comparative study required the assistance of many public agencies, private organizations and firms, and private individuals. Hundreds of interviews were conducted, several dozen public meetings were attended, and a mountain of articles and other documents were reviewed. Countless trips to each community were required to keep pace with the progress of each proposal. The formidable problems of following the course of three separate new community proposals over several years and selecting important features of each project could not have been overcome without the cooperation of local residents, staff members of the development firms, and employees of public agencies.

This is an exploratory effort, and it should be viewed as such. Using the concepts and methods of social science, I have attempted to offer insights into a subject area where none was previously available. As a practicing architect and city planner I participated in controversies over land development as an adversary to community residents. My later acquisition of special skills and a Ph.D degree in social science equipped me to view the emergence of controversy over land development as an observer with previous experience as a participant. A personal involvement in the earliest stages of the Lysander project as a city planner raised questions in my mind about how the proposal was being handled and the reasons for the emergence of controversy. Quite by coincidence members of my family, living in the Rochester area, brought the two proposals for Gananda and Riverton to my attention. The opportunity to study three proposals under different types of sponsorship (public and private) in similar settings and operating simultaneously was the inviting prospect being offered. As an environmental designer I felt that I could understand the developers' motives and strategies; as a social scientist I felt that I could examine the interactions of the involved participants. This adjustment across interdisciplinary lines is not an easy one, but is vitally important if participants in the urban development process are to understand each other's positions.

It is my hope that this work will contribute to an understanding of the way cities are built and help to reduce community conflict in regard to urban development.

I am indebted to many people for their assistance during the preparation of this book. I wish to express my appreciation to Ephraim Mizruchi, especially, and to Charles Willie, Alan K. Campbell, Louise Taylor, Guthrie Birkhead, and Clifford L. Winters, Jr., of Syracuse University for their advice and support during preparation of the original research.

Marion Clawson's *Suburban Land Conversion in the United States*, published by The Johns Hopkins University Press in 1971, has been important to my work. The late Hollister Kent was an inspirational influence in the development of the issues I addressed, and I remain indebted to him. Many members of the development corporations provided information: William Marcus and Irwin Davis of Lysander, Robinson Lapp of Gananda, and Scott Carlson of Riverton were particularly helpful in this regard.

Several publishers have granted me permission to use material from their books. Macmillan Publishing Co., Inc., granted permission to quote from James S. Coleman, *Community Conflict*, copyright 1957 by The Free Press. The M.I.T. Press gave permission to reprint Ebenezer Howard's figure from p. 46 of his *Garden Cities of To-Morrow*, Copyright 1965 by The M.I.T. Press. The Center for Urban and Regional Studies, The University of North Carolina at Chapel Hill, gave permission to use two tables from *Residential Developer Decisions—A Focused View of the Urban Growth Process* by Shirley F. Weiss, John E. Smith, Edward J. Kaiser, and Kenneth B. Kenney (1966; reprinted 1974).

Encouragement and critical editing were gratefully received from Dorothy Sickles. I am deeply obligated to Mina F. Pembroke for her diligent collection of material over the years and for providing a perspective of the local residents' feelings about the proposed developments.

The completion of the research over an extended period required the understanding of my wife, Linda. The book was written on her time; without her encouragement and support, it might not have reached final form.

HARVEY H. KAISER

Syracuse, New York

Contents

Tables

Figures and Maps

Abbreviations

ACIR	Advisory Commission on Intergovernmental Relations
CAC	Community Advisory Committee
HOCA	Greater Baldwinsville Homeowners' and Civic Association
HUD	United States Department of Housing and Urban Development
MDA	Metropolitan Development Association
PUD	Planned Unit Development
PNRS	Project Notification and Review System
SMSA	Standard Metropolitan Statistical Area
SURC	Syracuse University Research Corporation
UDC	New York State Urban Development Corporation

THE BUILDING OF CITIES

1 | Development and Conflict

The founding of new cities and the rebuilding or enlarging of the old have created some of the most exciting chapters in history. In preindustrial societies, communities developed physically, socially, and economically over decades and centuries. In contemporary societies, subject to industrialization and urbanization, the process of urban development is intensified. Individual and group interests tend to be sharply defined, and disagreement between parties can erupt into open community conflict that can be disruptive to the social and economic well-being of a community.

The notion of building a "new town" is as old as recorded history. Biblical kings, Greek philosophers, and Roman emperors built new settlements for religious, commercial, or defensive reasons. Hanseatic princes, Renaissance thinkers, and explorer-kings followed similar paths. Eighteenth- and nineteenth-century social philosophers pursued the idea, believing it a way to overcome the dehumanizing urban conditions created by industrialization. More recently, national governments have supported the creation of new towns as a means of achieving national economic and social goals. Emphasis has traditionally been placed on the design of the new community: its physical configuration, social and economic activities, and political organization. Little or no attention has been given to the people living or owning property at the site of the new development. What happens to them and why and how they react as they do is what this book is about.

The broader question we are asking is who controls the development of land? Is it the private property owner or the community? These unsettling questions have increasingly provoked controversy in urban and rural America. Various members of a community have widely divergent attitudes toward the development of land: the recent arrival seeks a residence to satisfy personal and family styles; the owner of developable land is concerned with gaining maximum personal financial benefit from future use of his holdings; the merchant and industrialist seek locations enabling them to maximize profits; established residents wish to preserve the qualities that influenced their decision to live there. And so on.

Particularly since the 1960's, the many individuals who have a stake in the outcome of land-development plans have been active in expressing their opinions. While it is true that public discussion which results in a consensus for action is vital to the future life of a community, violent disagreement about land development can cause irreparable damage to future relationships among community members. Citizens who strongly oppose a change in zone for a land developer will harbor bitterness against those who support change in the community. And how the publicly elected representatives and appointed officials respond to these cross-pressures affects the future quality of the community.

But the vital question of responsibility for decisions on land control has not been dealt with adequately. While statistics on urban sprawl, wastefulness of resources, and deteriorating quality of life are abundant, decisions on such diverse problems as consumption of land around the edges of the cities, dwindling fuel supplies, and damage to the environment require public action based on an understanding of the forces that create and change cities. During the first half of the history of the United States a largely agrarian nation held to a strong belief in the inviolability of private property rights. With the transition to an urban society, our regulatory and service institutions have had to change their concepts concerning the control of land development.

Conflict over land development is not limited to major urban centers where intense activities foster rapid change. Throughout the nation, whether urban or rural, issues such as zoning, highway location, the building of public facilities like schools, or the placement of utility lines arouse conflict. The small community remote from urban concerns can find itself in the midst of turmoil brought about by purely local issues. Or national policies toward the environment can bring about changes in local activities—for example, by controlling how gravel is extracted or how a local industry disposes of its wastes.

I will discuss here the process of urban development and the issue of land-development responsibility—the who, what, when, where, and how of public goals and policies—and specific aspects of the process. The general discussion is from a perspective that views the various elements of city building as interactive forces. Moving from the general to the specific, I will also consider the development of new communities and the conflicts both there and in older communities that arise when proposals are made for land development.

The Central Issues of Change

Change in a community can be social, economic, political, or physical, in one or a combination of these forms. Events surrounding physical change—which involves modification of the natural or man-made environment—provide a source for examining controversies within communities. Contrasted with social or political change—which deals with behavioral aspects of attitudes, beliefs, and values of individuals and organizations—physical change has a visible expression in the process of urban development.

Changes in the physical shape of communities are occurring in increasingly more dramatic and extensive ways. Some occur in an atmosphere of harmony and general consensus, while others stir bitter controversy. Both reactions can establish patterns that shape the future actions of the community. Changes in physical form are part of the complex process called urban development, which by its nature directly affects the lives and financial resources of many individuals in the community. As the complexities of an urban society increase, so do the comprehensiveness, size, and cost of projects. Negative reaction to development, including organized opposition, can disrupt a community by the way in which it modifies the social relationships of individuals and organizations in a community; the disruption can also accumulate excessive financial costs to the parties who may be expected to benefit from the proposal for change.[1]

Ideas for changing the physical environment of a community are embodied in the statements and presentations of individuals, entrepreneurs, public agencies, or government.[2] The suggestions may arise from sources indigenous to a community or from an outside source. In either case, the proposal can take a variety of forms ranging from a utopian generalization to a highly detailed statement supported by technical and financial analyses. The initiation of an idea is part of the process of urban development and its presentation can at once generate conflict within a community. This particular juncture is critical in the "setting in motion" of a conflict, for beyond this point controversies follow similar patterns—often a path that bears little relation to the beginnings of the idea.[3]

1. In our context the process of innovation is symbolized by the actions of the innovator and the reaction of the recipients toward a plan for the construction of physical improvement: e.g., housing, highways, community facilities. The issue which may or may not develop into controversy is sometimes summarized in a single document in the form of a proposal or charter describing goals, objectives, and details of the organization and methods of implementing. The process is discussed in R. Lippitt, J. Watson, B. Westley, The Dynamics of Planned Change (New York: Harcourt, Brace and World, 1958), pp. 1–89; A. Niehoff, A Casebook of Social Change (Chicago: Aldine, 1966), pp. 1–41; Everett M. Rogers, The Diffusion of Innovations (New York: Free Press, 1962).

2. The idea or proposal for change is a process that begins with a concept on the part of an entrepreneur and ends in its adoption or rejection by the community or potential community. Crain et al, described the process as starting with informal discussions of an idea as the initial stage. This is followed in succession by the stages of formulating a plan of action and seeking additional and broader support (proposal); the formal presentation to the body empowered to take action (presentation); the period in which arguments and pressures are focused on the decision-making body (action); and then the actual choice among possible outcomes (decision). Robert L. Crain, Elihu Katz, and Donald B. Rosenthal, The Politics of Community Conflict: The Fluoridation Decision (New York: Bobbs-Merrill, 1969), p. 53. Rogers' investigation of the recipient's adoption process for sociocultural change can be applied to the proposal phase of urban development. He lists five stages in the adoption process: (1) awareness; (2) interest; (3) evaluation; (4) trial; and (5) adoption. See Rogers, Diffusion of Innovations, pp. 81–86.

3. James S. Coleman, Community Conflict (New York: The Free Press, 1957), p. 9. One of the peculiarities of controversies noted by Coleman are the dynamics that cause the original issue to be diffused into the context of prior community activities.

Proposals for physical change provide ample source material for studies of community conflict as precipitated by external events. Studies of urban renewal and of highway plans that were brought to the level of controversy have become common in the professional literature of the behavioral and social sciences. However, these case studies are part of a literature generally lacking an initial framework for investigation in the form of a methodology, thus preventing re-evaluation of future events, or comparability with similar studies.

My specific goals here are: (1) to develop an understanding of the progressive stages in emerging controversy over planning proposals for urban development; and (2) to suggest theories as to the causes of different community reactions to change. The steps, or continuous action, which occur from the time a developer conceives of developing land until a project is under construction, involve the actors in the situation, the relationships between them, and the general social climate in which they exist. In each case we should be aware of (1) the characteristics of the actors involved; (2) the set of relations between the actors; and (3) the actors' environment or social context. We should clearly understand who and what the individuals or groups are and what they represent, if we are to understand their role in the land-development process. The retired farmer, who owns large land-holdings, will certainly view development differently than will the young exurbanite family. Similarly, the relations between them influence responses to development proposals. Would the farmer seeking supplemental retirement income, for instance, be concerned over preservation of environmental values? Finally, the social context of the issue, encompassing community attitudes and values, affects the emergence of controversy over development proposals.

In this volume, consideration of different community reactions to change is centered on: (1) the leadership of the community and the developer; (2) the kind of organization proposing the development; (3) the way the proposal is presented to the community; (4) the response of the local bureaucracy to the proposal; and (5) the influence of state and federal actions on the proposal. My conclusions are drawn from studies of three new-community-development projects in upstate New York: two near Rochester, and one near Syracuse. These studies were conducted over a three-year period by "living" with the projects, by regularly visiting each locale, by interviewing residents and developers, and by attending public meetings. In addition, public and private documents were reviewed in detail.

The new community or new town is one of several possible types of urban development. An attribute of the new community (as a type of urban development) is that the adoption stage is a distinct part of the process occurring in a defined time span. One of the distinguishing characteristics of new communities is the extremely large initial investment for a risky enterprise. Location and strength of market become more important for the large-scale, long-term new-community project than they are for other forms of development. These conditions require a well-formulated proposal for development, visibility of participants to increase public credibility and acceptance, and a strategy for presentation designed to gain support. Recent interest in new communities has been generated in America as a result of federal legislation in Title IV of the 1968 Housing and Urban Development Act (PL 90-448) and Title VII of the 1970 Housing and Urban Development Act (PL 91-609). This "new-town movement," has a lengthy international history with modern origins in Great Britain and Scandinavia. In America, the Greenbelt towns that originated in the Depression era through federal support in Maryland, Ohio, and Wisconsin are part of this heritage.

New-community proposals are characterized by the large scale of venture, involvement with multiple departments and agencies at different levels of government, relationships of an existing government to the new populations, and response of indigenous population to the "community builder." Decisions by the local government can assure success or failure in gaining approval, since support of public services, utilities, zoning, highways, and the tax considerations are vital to the developer. The three new-community proposals we will be discussing (see Figure 1.1) were in early planning stages concurrently in upstate New York in the late 1960's.

Lysander New Community is located north of Syracuse in the Town of Lysander, Onondaga County, and is the result of a proposal of the New York State Urban Development Corporation (referred to as UDC). This public agency has extraordinary powers under its Act of Incorporation, including complete independence

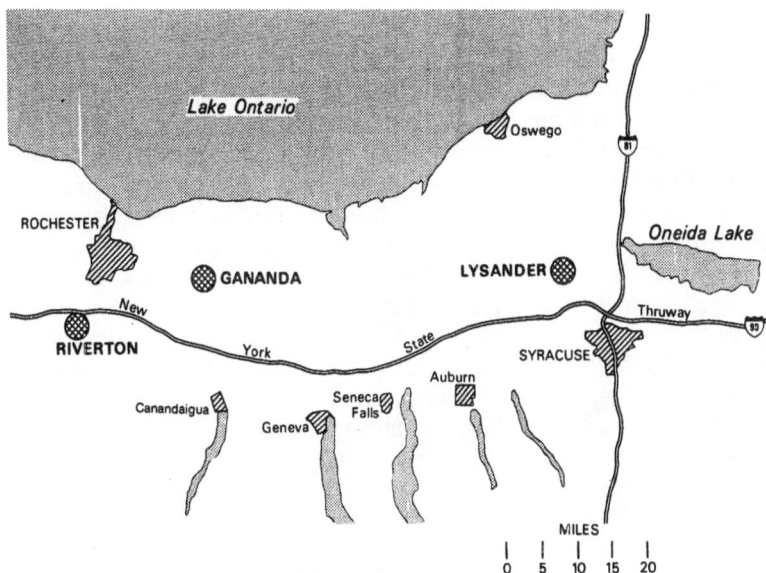

Figure 1.1. Map of new communities in upstate New York

from restrictions of local governments, although here and else-where considerable community controversy has centered on re-sistance to the agency's proposals. Lysander was the first publicly supported new community to receive federal support, and only one of two publicly supported projects of the fifteen approved through 1973. Gananda is a private new community in Wayne County, east of Rochester and was originally identified with its organizer, Stewart Moot. Land for this venture was purchased privately and lies in a mosaic of towns, villages, school districts, and other governmental units. The project began with local en-dorsement and a relative absence of controversy. Title VII ap-proval for the privately supported project was authorized in April, 1972. Construction started in the spring of 1973.

The third project, Riverton, is a new community in the Town of Henrietta, Monroe County, south of Rochester. Activities re-lated to the new community have been from private sources with personal identifications. Robert E. Simon (developer of Reston, Virginia, and recognized as instrumental in one of the first post-war United States "new towns") is publicly identified with the project. Howard E. Samuels and Harper Sibley, prominent local individuals, are also publicized as supporters of the project. In December, 1971, the United States Department of Housing and Urban Development (HUD) announced that Riverton was the seventh privately supported new-community proposal to be approved under Title VII. All three proposals are in similar stages of development, relatively similar in size, and in close geographic proximity. The social and economic setting of the three proposals are similar. Rochester and Syracuse, seventy-five miles apart, are basically conservative areas. Rochester is a regional center for a population of about 800,000, and Syracuse serves a region of about 650,000. Surrounding areas have highly productive agricultural activities, and each community is the home of nationally recognized manufacturing industries and colleges and universities. Incomes are above national levels, and unemployment runs below national trends.

Whereas the nature of the projects (all are new planned communities and all are in the same geographical area) is held constant, the following can be readily differentiated: leadership identity, source of proposal (public or private), and degree of controversy associated with each.

The central issues involved in controversy over development proposals deal with leadership, the nature of a project, and the environment of a project. Through observations provided by case studies, information on the importance and influence of certain factors on the dynamics of controversy may be assembled. The proliferation of studies concerned with community power or community leadership and the journalistic presentation of "how the bulldozer was stopped" do not provide answers for future guidance of social scientists and professional practitioners in environmental design fields. One of the simpler explanations for the failure of such studies is that the observers are limited to reporting and describing events. They need to look for answers to certain questions that arise about the emergence of controversy. For example, how does leadership in an organization proposing change minimize or maximize controversy? How does the source of a proposal, originating from either a private or a public agency, affect community reactions? Is the identification by the public of an individual representing leadership for a proposal a factor in the emergency of controversy? And how does the method in which a proposal is presented to a community influence possible conflict? These questions suggest three central issues on which to concentrate in understanding the emergence of controversy. The first area to consider is leadership, that is, the type of leadership evidenced by both the innovator and recipient of a plan for change.

Leadership[4]

In the search for an understanding of the forces at work in communities, researchers have examined the course of events in different situations to draw conclusions on the decision-making process. Part of this research has been directed toward questions of power: Who leads? How is leadership exercised? How do we identify the leaders? Studies of Middletown, Cibola, Yankee City, Springdale, and Levittown indicate that the personal and social characteristics of the advocates of change in a community are indicators for the emergence of controversy in a community. An exhaustive study of one type of controversy conducted at the University of Pennsylvania, concerning the location of public facilities, found that leadership was a fundamental force in the adoption process of urban development. A deduction reappearing in these studies relates leadership to the recipient's response to the project.

Of paramount importance to a community group is leadership. If the leadership does not have to answer to its community, if this leadership fails to generate new leadership, if it fails to make relevant assignments for its staff and task force, and if it shirks its own responsibilities for community improvement projects, then the community group will likely be ineffective. A good community leadership or lack of it will set the

4. Leadership will be discussed in the framework of types of authority defined by Weber as: (1) bureaucratic, (2) traditional, and (3) charismatic. See H. H. Gerth and C. W. Mills, *Max Weber: Essays in Sociology* (New York: Oxford University Press, 1946), pp. 224–229. Interpretations of Weber's theories on types of leadership are found in Reinhard Bendix, *Max Weber: An Intellectual Portrait* (Garden City, New York: Anchor Books, 1962), Part Three, chaps. 9–12. Several essays on the relationship of leadership to organizations, describing types of leadership, are in Amitai Etzioni, *Complex Organizations* (New York: Holt, Rinehart and Winston, 1964). Discussions on characteristics of leadership and relations to group performance that are considered basic to the subject are: Cecil Gibb, "Leadership," in Gardner Lindzey and Elliot Aronsin, eds., *Handbook of Social Psychology*, 2d ed. (Reading, Mass.: Addison-Wesley, 1968), pp. 877–917; and Dorwin Cartwright, *Group Dynamics*, 2d ed. (New York: Row, Peterson, 1960), pp. 487–509.

scene for community/agency discussions. When poor community leadership exists an agency can and will determine its own destiny in that community.[5]

One cannot discuss leaders apart from the groups they lead. A prominent leader or spokesman for a group is quickly identified by the communications media, and his name is then held in the forefront of any public discussion. This is useful, since a proposal can be more readily identified by the public in the form of a person than a faceless corporation. For example, a generally disliked sales tax in New York State is identified with Governor Nelson Rockefeller by reference to "Rocky's" tax. Similarly, construction proposals for major public works have become known by the skilled political entrepreneurs who directed the formation of administrative systems. The successes of the Port of New York Authority and New York's Triborough Bridge and Tunnel Authority, the United States Army Corps of Engineers, and the Tennessee Valley Authority are cases in point. At the core of these systems were skilled political entrepreneurs, such as Robert Moses, Austin Tobin, and Louis Danzig. It can be suggested that the identification of an organization with an individual indicates greater or lesser community confidence in success because of the visibility of a responsible individual with distinguishing characteristics.

The importance of individual attachments in the emergence of controversy is given a theoretical framework by James S. Coleman:

Individuals are seen as an aggregate of *attachments* of various kinds and strengths: attachments to persons, to groups, to beliefs or ideologies, to status, to power, etc. Each person is a particular configuration—unlike anyone else. This approach says three things: first, so far as we are concerned, other attributes of the individual—elements in his personality, etc.—are irrelevant; second, numerous things which have different names (values, relations to others, interest, attitudes, etc.) are all viewed alike, as *attachments;* third, these attachments act as "bridges" to relating the individual to new elements in his environment, and giving these

5. See the Discussion Paper Series, *Research on Conflict in Locational Decisions,* John Wolpert, Principal Investigator (Philadelphia: The Wharton School, University of Pennsylvania, 1970); and Barry Malko, *Notes on the Development of a Community Opposition Group* (Philadelphia: The Wharton School, University of Pennsylvania, 1970).

elements meaning. Depending on the relation he perceives his objects-of-attachment (persons, groups, values, etc.) to have to the new element, these existing attachments will lead him to develop a positive or negative attachment to the new element. His existing attachments act, in effect, as directives for action in new situations.[6]

The public attitude toward a leader as the symbol of a construction proposal can also be influenced by the organizational source of such a proposal. The two sources considered in this book are public (government) and private. The involvement of the public sector in urban development and redevelopment has been supported as constitutional by the courts, if not readily accepted at the local level. In a democratic society continually arguing the extension (or as some would have it, the encroachment) of government into the entrepreneurial role, a community response may depend upon whether the proposal originates in the public or the private sector. The fact that the progress of a proposal for public improvements concludes with a public hearing implies that the public is granted the opportunity to reject such proposals. This rejection must be supported by clear evidence of general dissatisfaction with a scheme, a condition that often results after emergence of an issue into community conflict.

For example, the unexpectedly strong community resistance and ultimate rejection of a housing proposal by the New York State Urban Development Corporation in Westchester County precipitated a thorough investigation into local response to governmental involvement in development concepts.[7] UDC's survey produced conclusive evidence that private sponsorship was preferable to public initiation of a project. Furthermore, the higher the level of government involved, the less desirable the proposal. The issue of "home rule" is prominent in this argument. Threats to municipal sovereignty were of focal concern by opponents of the Urban Development Corporation.

These conclusions reflect residents' fears of changes which they believed would be induced by governmental intervention, such as fears of urbanization, deterioration, and the destruction of a pleasant, suburban environment; racial fears, including the feel-

6. Coleman, *Community Conflict*, pp. 25–26.
7. Oliver Quayle and Co., *A Survey of Attitudes toward Government Assisted Moderate and Low Income Housing in Westchester County, New York*, Study #1546 (mimeographed; December, 1972).

ing that blacks don't need further help; anxieties over increased crime and drug abuse (which are closely related to fears of blacks), fears of higher property taxes (an apprehension which could be alleviated by having the state reimburse each community for loss of tax revenue due to tax abatements); and fears of overcrowded schools and to a lesser degree fears of lowering the quality of local education.

Closely related to the negative attitude toward governmental intervention are the theories of alienation, supported repeatedly in studies of local politics and "political negativism." Robert L. Crain has summarized this issue by examining the causes of rejection of fluoridation proposals. From the psychological viewpoint, he believes rejection is due to a lack of personal connection to centers of power and decision-making.[8] With this attitude of the public in mind, one may properly question the appropriateness of placing development powers for comprehensive projects in the hands of a public body. The identification of the innovator with a governmental agency may predict a rate of rejection higher than if the identification was with a private source.

Nature of a Project and Individual Response

Individual attitudes toward the plan for development can also cause controversy. The second central issue, then, is concerned not only with the nature of a project plan, but individual responses to that plan.

When a proposal for urban development is first announced, it is often not clear to community residents how the project will actually affect them. Their reactions tend to be based on what have been called "initial determinants": their general attitude toward the proposal and their opinion of the group proposing change. These initial determinants of community attitudes are influenced, among other factors by the timing of the announcement, the residuum of past controversy, the content of the issue, and the area of life the proposal affects. The announcement is likely to provoke the hostility of some community groups regardless of when and how it is made. If the community is not informed of the proposed plans until the process of gaining official approval

8. Robert Crain et al., *The Politics of Community Conflict*, chap. 3.

is well advanced, the local government may be charged with trying to "sneak something over" on the residents, and opposition will be aroused because of the suddenness of the announcement. On the other hand, if the residents are informed early in the process, there will be time for groups to calculate their stakes and for opponents of the project to mobilize. Eventually, there will also be charges of delay or dishonesty, and outcries from owners and real estate men who have economic issues at stake.

The formation of individual attitudes toward a plan for development starts after the first awareness of a project. Individuals and groups calculate what they will gain or lose if the project is approved. They consider the kinds of stakes—economic, political, and social—they have in the area and what effect the project will have on these stakes. The calculation of gain or loss is the most important determinant of their attitude.

Individual participation in controversy has been attributed in part to a person's attitudes toward a plan: the individual's sense of relative impotence, degree of political awareness, and knowledge about the functioning of political processes. The degree and depth of political knowledge does not affect reaction to a project plan; the crucial predictor tends to be the economic stake of property ownership by the individual. It has been found repeatedly that the level of participation depends upon the level of knowledge about a particular project and on the sense of threat that is implied by this understanding.[9]

The amount of information about a project that is revealed to the public influences formation of attitudes. Typically, plans presented in terms of general goals and community-wide benefits are more likely to be accepted than those posed in terms of individual threats and costs. James W. Wilson has maintained that

The view which a neighborhood is likely to take of urban renewal, then, is in great part a product of its class composition. Upper- and upper-

9. This conclusion has been reached in all studies of resistance to change. Surveys conducted in works such as Julian Wolpert's *Research on Conflict*, Clarence Davies' work, *Neighborhood Groups in Urban Renewal* (New York: Columbia University Press, 1960), and the Quayle and Co. study for UDC support this view. Descriptions of events in Cambridge by Gordon Fellman conclude that "a direct threat had to be present before people could mobilize. It would take important and explicitly defined action to get the residents aroused." See Malko, *Notes on the Development*, p. 35.

middle-class people are more likely to think in terms of general plans, the neighborhood or community as a whole, and long-term benefits (even when they might involve immediate costs to themselves); lower- and lower-middle class people are more likely to see such matters in terms of specific threats and short-term costs.[10]

Officials find themselves in a quandary as they try to determine the extent of detail that should be presented to the public. Efforts to deal with reducing opposition require fully detailed plans in anticipation of controversy, although full disclosure requires a strategy for responding to emerging controversy.

A brief summary of the economic, political, social, and ideological stakes involved may lead toward an understanding of an individual's attitude to a project plan.

Economic Stakes. The economic stakes of various segments of a community are the most visible and perhaps the most influential in determining attitudes of certain groups. Plans for physical development involve the use of land, and land use affects two distinct groups: one with direct interests in property, the other with indirect interests. Those with direct interests include home-owners, institutions owning property, real estate agents, tenants, and financial sources. Groups affected after the first transaction of events are the construction industry, local government, and community institutions. Probably the strongest support for controversy comes from homeowners, although they are not necessarily the leadership. This group has both an economic and emotional investment in the community. Two pressing questions for the homeowner are: What will this plan do to my property values? and What will this plan do to my taxes? Much of the controversy in small-town or suburban community politics is concerned with little else.[11]

Political Stakes. There are three general categories of persons whose attitudes toward a proposed project will be influenced largely by the political effects which they think the project will have. ("Political" is here used in the broad sense of that which affects power rather than in the narrow sense of partisan poli-

10. James W. Wilson, "Citizen Participation in Urban Renewal," *Journal of the American Institute of Planners*, 29:4 (Nov., 1963), 242–249.
11. Robert C. Wood, *Suburbia: Its People and Their Attitudes*, (Boston: Houghton Mifflin, 1958), pp. 161–197; Arthur Vidich and Joseph Bensman, *Small Town in Mass Society* (Princeton: Princeton University Press, 1958), pp. 109–136.

tics.) These three categories are partisan political leaders, positional leaders, and institutional leaders.

For partisan political leaders, the major determinant is the attitude of their constituencies. The relationship between politicians and their constituencies is modified by several factors. First, the politicians must consider what proportion of their constituencies will be affected by the project and how deeply they will be affected. Second, they must take into account the kind of organization that supports them. How soon the politicians or their associates have to run for office is a third factor.

The positional leaders of business and local government are the two major groups that exercise power in American communities. Involvement of these leaders in a controversy occurs when their bases of power are at issue. The primary objective of positional leaders is the maintenance and enhancement of position.

Institutional leaders, such as ministers, school principals, and community agency officials often have a stake in maintaining the existing situation in the community. For them, variables such as autonomy and subsequent risk of loss of job, their identity with a community, and the degree of centralization of policy-making are factors that influence their attitudes toward a project proposal and the roles they might play in support of or opposition to the project.

Social Stakes. People may lose economically or politically by having their environment altered, and they may also lose socially. The concept of social loss as a stake in determining attitudes can be explained by the reciprocal relations between the individual, family, or group, and the urban environment. William Michelson's perspective on the environment and its effects are tabulated as a series of pathologies: the city itself, housing conditions, traffic, and the physical environment all combine to cause abnormal activities.[12] He has summarized that "the surest way to induce pathological responses in people through environmental manipulation is to force their move from a neighborhood which is congruent with their life styles without either a substitute life style desired on their part or a physically acceptable neighborhood open for their mass relocation." This modification in the status quo of a social system inspires a sense of loss that is

12. William Michelson, *Man and His Urban Environment* (Reading, Mass.: Addison-Wesley, 1970), chap. 3.

expressed as fear of or hostility toward change. When people have been forced to change their residence, the result under certain circumstances has been what psychiatrists call a "grief syndrome." The concept of social loss is measured against the maintenance of a social system. Herbert Gans found that Boston's West Enders suffered such loss as a result of redevelopment. He says that "for tenants, owners, and businessmen alike, the destruction of the neighborhood exacted social and psychological losses. The clearance destroyed not only buildings, but also a functioning social system."[13]

Ideological Stakes. Less visible than economic, political, or social stakes in forming attitudes are ideological stakes. Individuals may be motivated by the ideas they hold even when these ideas are not directly related to the more concrete issues they contend with in the political arena. For example the fluoridation issue was seen by some observers as an ideological matter, although sometimes confused with political alienation.[14] By making a distinction between the two, Crain and others showed that a determinant of attitudes is the ideological position. There is danger of converting ideology into a residual category to explain all actions not easily attributable to the other kinds of stakes we have discussed. Ideas do move people to action, however, and we cannot fully analyze the attitudes of community groups without taking account of the ideological factors at work.

Environment of the Proposal

Further issues involved in attitudes toward change originate from the environment or context of the proponents and recipients of a planning proposal. Coleman and Louis Kriesberg viewed the environment of adversaries in a controversy in a social context[15] and noted that differences in the social and economic structure of the community affect the course of controversy. Coleman concluded that communities which were highly socially integrated tended to absorb conflict, and controversy was thus minimized. Those communities lacking ties between individuals and groups

13. Herbert Gans, *The Urban Villagers* (New York: The Free Press, 1962), p. 320.

14. See, generally, Robert L. Crain et al., *The Politics of Community Conflict*, chap. 3.

15. Coleman, *Community Conflict*, pp. 18–25; Louis Kriesberg, *Sociology of Social Conflicts* (Englewood Cliffs, N.J.: Prentice-Hall, 1973), pp. 95–98.

increased conflict beyond absorption to the point at which permanent cleavages were created. The community's economic structure can ameliorate or exacerbate discord—summarized in the following fashion:

The effects of the community's economic structure in inhibiting or promoting community conflict have been treated under other headings. At this point it is useful to summarize these effects on the three economic variations noted: "service" towns in which townspeople derive their income from outsiders; "self-contained" towns, in which men both live and work; and economic "appendages," in which most men commute to work outside town.

(a) In each of these, characteristic issues arise to provoke controversy. In economically self-contained towns, it is often issues of direct economic interest and of political control; in the others it is more often value differences deriving from differing backgrounds and experiences.

(b) In the stratified, self-contained communities, participation in the controversy will ordinarily be restricted to the upper and middle strata, while in the one-class commuting towns it will be more evenly spread throughout the community.

(c) When lower classes participate in controversy in stratified towns, the dispute is likely to get particularly acrimonious.

(d) The voluntary aspect of relations among residents who need only to live together and not to work together—in new suburbia—tends to segregate the community into discrete value-homogeneous groups, and to create diverse consequences for controversy.[16]

Kriesberg views the environment of adversaries as a force influencing identities, grievances, and goals.[17] The prevailing ways of thinking at any given time profoundly affect the categories by which people think of themselves. Identification in terms of values, attitudes, and beliefs may be more or less salient in different times and places. Grievances within a social context describe general differences between groups, which may or may not escalate to controversy. Goals include the formulated aims of a social structure. The visibility of different groups in a society makes it easy for any group to recognize its adversaries.

External to the adversaries' characteristics are the portrayals

16. Coleman observed that the ability of the social structure of a community to avoid controversy is complicated when such a factor as the economic structure of the community is working against integration (*Community Conflict*, p. 23).

17. Kriesberg, *Sociology of Social Conflicts*, p. 95.

created by mass media. A subject well scrutinized in recent presidential campaigns, the effect of the media on generating controversy has been assigned varying degrees of importance by different observers of community conflict. The presence of similar or related events in a community's history can be used by the media to transform latent public opinion into a position of active opposition. Past controversies will influence the attitude taken toward a proposed plan, because the various groups involved will view the proposal in the context of other issues that had previously divided the community or had set the community against the project supporter.

Approaching the Issues

My reasons for looking into the building of cities—to understand the activities within a community that occur when a planning proposal is presented and the processes that are involved in the emergence of conflict over a planning proposal—have affected the selection of methodology. The models chosen for this investigation are similar to those found in Arthur Vidich's and Joseph Bensman's *Small Town in Mass Society*, in Gans's *Urban Villagers* and *The Levittowners*.[18] These authors rely heavily on participant observation, although they are cautious in their use of this research tool.

As noted earlier, a good deal of time was spent looking into the overall situation in the three communities to get a "feeling" for each of the prospective communities. Field visits provided familiarity with local characteristics of the proposed sites and an introduction to local attitudes; and contacts with project managers for each of the three proposed new communities provided information on the substantive aspects of each proposal.[19] A search of newspaper articles outlined the progress of

18. The method is documented in appendixes both authors have attached to their studies. See Vidich and Bensman, *Small Towns in Mass Society*, pp. 348–396; Gans, *The Urban Villagers*, pp. 336–350; and Gans, *The Levittowners* (New York: Pantheon Press, 1963). Colin Bell and Howard Newby in *Community Studies* (New York: Praeger, 1971) devote a chapter to "Community Study as a Method of Empirical Investigation," pp. 54–81. Readers interested in seeking further information on the authors' reservations and qualifications should examine these references.

19. Preliminary interviews in the fall of 1972 with the three project managers were held with Scott Carlson of Riverton, Robinson Lapp of Gananda, and William Marcus of Lysander.

each proposal with references to significant actions and the role of leading personalities, and an examination of public records summarized community response to a proposal and recorded the actions of responsible public officials. Participant observation of public meetings and other community bodies assisted in recording evidence of resistance to change. Interviews conducted in each community with sponsor representatives, elected representatives, and others, introduced the personal viewpoint.

Making use of these various opportunities for observation and the data they supplied, I constructed a set of working hypotheses. The general hypothesis that the type of leadership has a direct influence on the community response to a proposed project for physical development leads to the following propositions:

1. In any situation involving planned change, the degree of controversy varies according to the type of leadership.
2. The potential for community adoption of a development plan increases with identification of the project with an individual rather than a group.
3. Identification of a project with a public body decreases possibilities of acceptance. The degree of acceptance is proportional to the level of government, highest for local, and lowest for federal.
4. Identification of a project with a private group decreases the chance for emergence of controversy.
5. The greater the stake of the strong community leader in maintaining the status quo of the social or political system, the greater the opposition to change.
6. Project leadership and decision-making in the hands of technicians without evidence of backing by local political leaders decrease the chance of local acceptance.

With respect to the influence of individual attitudes on controversy, the following propositions seem appropriate:

7. Plans presented in terms of general goals and community-wide benefits have a greater chance of acceptance than those that pose threats to individuals in terms of changed environment and excessive costs.
8. The level of participation and the intensity of citizen participation are dependent upon the level of knowledge about a particular project, and on the sense of threat implied by this understanding.
9. Partial presentation, in contrast to complete plans or factual

errors, increases community opposition and sustains controversy.

10. Objections to a project plan have a greater chance of creating and sustaining controversy when issues are procedural and not substantive.
11. The greater the vested interest in an area affected by a plan, the higher the incidence of opposition.
12. Involvement of property owners in opposing a plan is directly influenced by their perception of the effects of the project on property values and taxes.
13. Power groups will intervene in controversy when their bases of power are the issue.
14. The major determinant of a partisan political leader's attitude toward a plan are the attitudes of his constituency.

And, finally, propositions developed from a consideration of the effect of the environment or social context on adversaries are:

15. The greater the economic differentiation in a community, the greater the possibilities of controversy over a project proposal.
16. The greater the social stratification in a community, the greater the possibility of controversy over a project proposal.
17. A community with a past history of controversy over physical development will be predisposed toward controversy in future events.
18. Events totally external to the project proposal but influencing local attitudes, beliefs and values, can create opposition to a plan.

Conceiving working hypotheses at the inception will allow them to be surrendered for better ones. In addition, having the hypotheses available for comparison with the proposal sponsor's interpretation of local opposition in each community sets up additional theories for evaluation.

Architects, landscape architects, engineers, urban planners—all involved in the process of design and construction of the urban environment—should benefit from the opportunity to apply theories of resistance to change. Steps can be incorporated into the urban design and highway planning processes which can avoid conflict and possible rejection of proposals. Social scientists concerned with the impact of two factors—the adoption process and the man-made environment—on behavioral characteristics can apply their theories to developing predictive and analytical tools of research. Those social science fields such as political science and sociology can shift their concern from maintenance of certain standards of political and social functions to investigations of alternative preference. Michelson has stressed this responsibility by endorsing involvement of the social scientist in studying productively how certain kinds of people adjust to the various kinds of environments that exist today. He says that "in short, social scientists can produce informed estimates of the spatial needs of future construction as a result of their present studies, providing that they study human behavior in conjunction with the most basic concepts of space. This will aid experts in design by enabling them to concentrate on the most desirable means to the spatial ends."[20]

By knowing more about the conditions that lead to controversy, the designer of the physical environment will be better able to foresee the consequences of his decisions and to consider such conditions as criteria in the decision-making process for public improvement locations. Thus it is possible that much of the loss of resources spent on combating public opposition, or on the development of plans that cannot be implemented, could be prevented.

By studying several examples of proposals for change in the physical structure of communities it becomes possible to come "to grips with social and psychological facts in the raw." As more light is shed upon the processes of change and as empirical evidence is gathered, it becomes possible to predict events and activities that will encourage consensus and integration.

Summary

Participation in a controversial proposal for urban development—be it a zoning ordinance, housing project, or other alteration to a community fabric—can be an unnerving experience. It can also be financially expensive, politically disastrous, and/or contribute to irreparable damage to a community. What are the forces that contribute to dissent? Can they be identified prior to emergence of a conflict situation? These questions, which form

20. Michelson, *Man and His Urban Environment*, p. 203.

the basis of the working hypotheses, introduce a new dimension to the study of community conflict, where previous investigations have varied in subject matter, units of analysis, and methodology. A specific examination of the role, character, and functional activities of the leaders in community conflict in relation to urban development will supplement those previously prepared.

Two potential limitations for the findings set forth in this book should be pointed out: the first is related to future use for comparative purposes, and the second to an understanding of the phenomenon of new communities. Selection of three locations in upstate New York may be thought to limit the findings to the geographical, historical, and cultural aspects of that area. The procedures that are used here, however, may be applicable to other settings, and the conclusions valid for comparing this type of development to similar proposals.

The potential impact of new communities on American society is of enormous magnitude. Billions of dollars can be funneled into the program through federal guarantees and financial assistance, and complementary expenditures by other public bodies, and private enterprise could equal or exceed the national investment. The social issues raised by new communities will influence the lives of individuals and existing communities for generations. For each new community, then, an understanding of the proposal for change and of the factors conditioning acceptance is of great importance for policy makers, technicians, and representative leadership.

Urban land development can be viewed from the historic perspective of urbanization in the United States. The movement of population and the flow of people to the cities have altered social values and created new attitudes toward land development. Changes in community attitudes and in individual values are mirrored in the judicial and legislative response toward land policies that protect the property rights of communities and individuals under pressure by development. The process of land development has a direct effect on individual attitudes and the emergence of community conflict.

2 | City Building

The process of urban development and the ensuing emergence of community conflict are not phenomena unique to industrialized societies. However, the rate of urbanization in the United States in the past five decades has created greater stress on traditional relationships of the individual, the community, and land development than previously experienced. If the United States were a static or declining nation, the likelihood of controversies relating to land development would be minimal. The dynamic nature of an industrializing and urbanizing nation in a free-enterprise economy creates problems that prevail in communities throughout the nation in urban, suburban, and rural settings.

In this chapter we will review the interacting forces in an urbanizing society that form the framework for community conflict. Our purpose here is to examine the process of urban development and those groups involved in the decision-making process. In the process of selecting which new communities to consider (in a study such as this one) as specific forms of comprehensive urban land development questions arise about the contextual factors for decisions in the development process. For example: What factors provide the environment for developer and community decision-making? What are the characteristics of the decision agents in the process? In addition to these questions, we will explore the interaction between the decision agents.

The fact which becomes evident here is how little we know about the process of comprehensive urban development or about the individuals who initiate the action. Ideally, one should have information on the personal profiles of the individuals concerned—their age, education, income, wealth, status, and other measurable socioeconomic characteristics. Still more useful would be information on their mental and emotional processes—on "what makes them tick." As a body of knowledge such as ours accumulates, we can come to a firmer understanding of the determinants and influence of participants involved in the process of urban land development.

Urbanization

The process of urbanization described by population shifts and socioeconomic disparities is the focus of the "urban problem" in the United States. Concern for the problem led to creation of the Douglas Commission (the National Commission on Urban Problems), which was charged specifically "to recommend the solutions . . . to increase the supply of low-cost decent housing," although its public hearings and study reports have, more widely, explored areas relevant to urban land development and controversial aspects of the subject. A wealth of data was collected, and its report, *Building the American City*,[1] assists in interpreting the thrust of contemporary American social goals and values in relation to individual and community attitudes toward urban land development.

Disparities in socioeconomic aspects of urbanization have also received attention from the Advisory Commission on Intergovernmental Relations (ACIR). Urbanization and policies for future growth were examined and reported on in *Urban and Rural America*,[2] and provided conclusive recommendations for new communities. I have drawn heavily on both the Douglas Commission reports and the work of the ACIR.

1. 91st Congress, 1st Session, *Building the American City*, Report of the National Commission on Urban Problems (Washington, D.C., 1968). The Commission was established by Congress (PL 380, 1959) to give attention to intergovernmental problems, and its members are representatives from federal, state, and local governments.
2. Advisory Commission on Intergovernmental Relations, *Urban and Rural America* (Washington, D.C., April, 1968).

Patterns of Urbanization. The change from a predominantly rural to predominantly urban America occurred about five decades ago. By 1970 over 70 percent of the population lived in urban places; in 1920 just over 50 percent lived in urban areas. The rapid growth created several paradoxes: the emergence of an urban nation in a country that has a rural bias against cities; greater urban growth, but a loss of population dominance by older center cities; dynamic expansion emerging in broad geographic crescents that involve regions and states which until recently had a strong antiurban tradition; large and small enclaves of highly differentiated socioeconomic and racial groups forming a heterogeneous composition of urban areas; and an inconsistent pattern of physical development at the periphery of expanding urban areas that is described as "sprawl."

The devastating effects of urban society on man, his institutions, and the natural environment, have been of long-standing concern to American intellectuals from Jefferson to Emerson to Dewey—whose philosophy in a sense celebrates the pluralism of American urban life. The broad and articulate base of support for the urban development critique has strongly influenced the acceptance of new communities, creating an atmosphere in which the objectives of the new communities are seen as matters of public concern.

The hortatory language of the critics of urban development dwells for the most part on the disorderly patterns created on the urban perimeter. Urban sprawl is frequently the cause of arguments over developers' proposals in suburban areas, and objection to sprawl is invoked in support of new communities. The Environmental Protection Agency's 1974 study, *Costs of Sprawl*,[3] summarized the case against sprawl in the following way:

(1) a sprawled or continuous urban development is more costly and less efficient than a compact one; (2) sprawl is unesthetic and unattractive; (3) sprawl is wasteful of land since the intervening land is not specifically used for any purpose; (4) land speculation is unproductive, absorbing capital, manpower and entrepreneur skills without commensurate public gains; and (5) it is inequitable to allow a system in which the land occupier is required to shoulder such a heavy burden of capital charges or debt merely for site costs—costs which in large part are unnecessary and avoidable.

3. Environmental Protection Agency, *Costs of Sprawl* (Washington, D.C., 1974).

How do we reconcile this description of sprawl with the fact that suburbia is the residential preference of an increasing proportion of our society? Why do so many community conflicts over zoning controversies, highway construction, and other disruptions arise in an environment characterized by sprawl? One observer answers:

For all the course of protests, however, most Americans seem strangely unaroused. Each year they buy a few hundred thousand picture windows, feed a few hundred thousand more lawns. The decay of the central city barely concerns them; the cries of strangling congestion stirs them only briefly; even the issue of mounting taxes, an exposed nerve in the structure of local politics, does not seem to have the capacity to bring them shouting into the streets. . . . The striking disparity between the literature of protests and the lethargy of the citizen is a riddle which demands an answer. What I shall contend in substance is that the clear majority of Americans who live in urban areas look on their lifetime experience as one of progress and improvement not as retrogression; that they see their lot as being better than that of their parents and confidently expect the children to do a little better still.[4]

In seeking explanations of the fervor expressed by opponents of change in the urban perimeter, we need to understand the phenomenon of suburbanization (with sprawl as one of its unfortunate results).

Suburbanization. Movement of population as a factor in the urbanization of the United States is marked by two elements—population concentration on a national scale, and population decentralization on a metropolitan scale. Data from the 1970 Census showed that suburban areas contained a greater percentage of population than central city or rural areas. The most striking and important aspect of the population redistribution has been not only its numbers, but its socioeconomic character. The dynamic nature of suburbanization (particularly the problems associated with change resulting from redistribution), constitutes a potential source of community conflict. The emphasis placed on population redistribution is indicated by the large number of scholarly investigations of the subject by economists, sociologists, political scientists, public administrators, and virtually every hyphenated discipline of the social sciences, whose studies indicate that the

4. Raymond Vernon, *The Myths and Reality of Our Urban Problems* (Cambridge, Mass.: Joint Center for Urban Studies, 1962).

major expansion of the American city can be attributed to the following: the conjunctive factors of population increase and family formation; the influence of categorical federal programs for housing and highway construction; location of available land for home building; shifts in job location; changes in transportation; and development of new modes of communication. Although these factors influence population distribution, more insight is needed into the attitudes and values of suburbanites when faced with change in their environment.

There are grounds for debating whether suburbanization is a specific and valid preference or merely a by-product of other preferences. Some persons believe improvements in transportation and communication merely make it possible for people to do what they have always wanted: to live in an environment with green space and air and sunshine yet keep their chances of making a living in the great metropolitan labor market. Others are less convinced of the validity of this position and see in the modern suburban movement a pincers action: people who want to escape some aspects of their present location and housing can find what they consider to be more desirable conditions only if they sacrifice locational convenience, time, and effort.

One of the reasons for moving to suburbia is the need for more spacious housing and the desire of people to own their own homes. Home ownership means, for most families, ownership of a single-family home. Furthermore, financial incentives toward purchase of a new detached dwelling support the process of suburbanization. Low initial down payments, income tax relief, and the expectation of protection against inflationary trends are elements that influence selection of individual homes in suburban locations. The effect of the fiscal environment through taxation policies, as reflected in quality and quantity of public services, underscores the important role of the economics of housing in influencing personal attitudes toward urban land development.

Robert Wood's basic study on the subject cites the ideology of rural living, often the theme of antiurbanists such as Mumford, as not the least of forces at work: "The image of small town life that every migrant held in his mind and that every real estate speculator raised as a conscious symbol. In some ways the ideal comprehended the forces which were at work . . . the desire for space, family life, and the homestead were part and parcel of the image itself."[5] Nevertheless, increasing population pressure has been and still is spoiling the dream. To stem population growth some suburban communities have reacted by applying land-use controls as protective devices that, in effect, build fences around the large central cities.

Impact of Urbanization. The widespread disparities between suburbia, central city, and rural areas illustrate the impact of urbanization on the fabric of life in the United States. Population mobility and migration have been identified as having pervasive effects on the community life of this country.

The President's *Report on National Growth* summarizes future problems likely to be associated with the process and patterns of urban land development as: (1) decline of rural areas and small towns; (2) a changed role for the central city; (3) racial and economic concentration; (4) environmental and transportation uncertainties; and (5) higher land costs. The magnitude and complexity of these problems have generally proven to be beyond the capabilities of local government. Thus, state and federal relief has been sought through legislative and judicial responses. As a result, state and federal actions are exerting direct influence on local activities in the fields of housing, land development, and land-use controls.

Urban Land Development: Social Values

When related to broader aspects of demography and societal trends, urban land development appears to be inextricably tangled in highly complex issues. Basic values of a democratic society are involved and can be the source of an initial, and sometimes enduring, community controversy. Important here are the relationships, including constitutional principles of due process, between government and individuals. In some instances the Fifth and Fourteenth Amendments, which were intended to protect individual rights, have been interpreted unjustly and have become a causative factor in creating conflicts.

A dynamic urban growth process often creates stress between the rights of the individual property owner and government. How does the individual property owner protect himself against

5. Robert C. Wood, *Suburbia: Its People and Their Politics* (Boston: Houghton Mifflin, 1958), p. 65.

loss of value due to the encroachment of another individual upon his enjoyment and pleasure? How does the community draw the line between the privilege of use and the interest of surrounding owners in the untrammeled use of their land? These questions affect basic legal rights and basic values in a democratic society.

Judicial treatment of conflicts arising from unplanned urban life—due to increased population pressures on diminishing quantities of land—is concerned with constitutional questions. Primarily, it involves four of the most important constitutional doctrines: (1) the due process clause, (2) the equal protection clause, (3) the rule against delegation of legislative power, and (4) the various rules affecting finality of administrative decisions. The doctrines of constitutional law can be regarded as codifications of basic social values, such as equal treatment before the law. The right of individuals or groups to be free from discrimination—on a racial, ethnic, or economic basis—is of particular significance for planning and for planning law. It is assumed that equal access to decent living conditions, and thus to the possibility of friendly contacts and the development of mutual respect among different groups, is a matter of major importance to the future social structure of our society. Legally, protections against discriminatory treatment by government are enforced by the equal protection clause. The enforcement of such rights often serves a higher social value, since it may help to establish the rights of groups otherwise unprotected, thus promoting the general public interest as well as the rights of individuals.

The dichotomy of land policies is evident in the formulation of regulations and in traditional American attitudes toward land development. Land speculation and land development have always been part of the American experience, representing a strong current in American history of individual land ownership largely unfettered by public control of its use. The lure of virgin land which encouraged early settlement, and the policies of "manifest destiny," were a dominant force in eighteenth- and nineteenth-century America. Traditions of speculation in real estate are early evidenced by a letter written in 1783, from Silas Deane to a friend, noting that "if we review the use and progress of private fortunes in America, we shall find that a very small proportion of them has arisen or been acquired by commerce, compared with

those made by the prudent purchase and management of land."[6]
Rampant speculation in land has moderated somewhat in the
twentieth century, but land retains the strong psychological
aspect of a source for quick and substantial wealth in the United
States.

Balanced against the speculative nature of real estate operations are those constitutional doctrines of due process and police
power. It is an accepted principle that the ownership of land is
exclusive but not absolute; each owner may use his property to
the exclusion of others, but he must use it with due respect to the
limitations imposed by society. Within the ambivalent attitude
toward urban land policies, the group, or community, has certain
rights in each parcel of land ownership that must be respected.
Thus, individual decisions of owners and investors for utilization
of the land are not completely free of restraints. The extent and
nature of the interest of the community in each parcel of ownership are ever changing in accordance with the evolving needs of
society.

A basic part of the American tradition of land development is
that it is first, last, and always a business operation conducted for
profit. The merit of any decision is always judged by its effect on
profit. Couched in the economists' terms, conflicts that arise between public and individual interest in land use are in some
cases the products of unwise business decisions, but more often
conflict arises because the individual viewpoint is not community-wide or sufficiently long-term. Orientation to the profit
motive too often results in short-term conclusions. Thus, land
may be exploited by overintensive development—which leads to
congestion and overcrowding, to slums, and to blight. Subdivisions may be inappropriately located or the land misused by
poor planning: small lots, inadequate public areas, or street systems unrelated to the street pattern of the central city. It is quite
probable that where land developers and builders seek a quick
profit rather than a long-term investment return, their interests
may run counter to the social good. In such cases, the original
exploitive profit to the developer-owner will be more than
equaled by detriments to future owners. Where a long-term in-

6. Edward P. Eichler and Marshall Kaplan, *The Community Builders* (Berkeley,
Calif.: University of California Press, 1967), p. 12.

vestment viewpoint is held, the interests of property owners and the community are less apt to be antagonistic.

The adjustments of the developers' goals and those of society to a point of congruity are necessarily incorporated in any concept for a new community, especially where the concept requires large land assemblage in economically favorable locations, coordination of public and private site improvements, and a desire of the developer to remain with a project over an extended period of time. It is likely that one of the explanations for antisocial exploitation or misuse of land can be found in the uncertainty of long-term investment in real estate, when, in some instances, as a result of these uncertainties, entrepreneurs have found it the wiser course to unload rather than to hold land for development. However, the new breed of developers, often called the "community builders," have attempted to create a degree of certainty in long-term investments by venturing into the more comprehensive land-development techniques of new communities. Implicitly a long-term commitment, the new-community concept brings together the goals of the developer with the social aim of rational policies for land development. This convergence would tend to minimize conflicts between public and individual interest in land use.

Although large-scale land assembly offers opportunities to achieve social values through the land-development process, negative effects cannot be overlooked. Potential for controversy emerges as landowners recognize that the value captured by the owner of large holdings may threaten the loss of value increment for others in the area. The problem of land value change resulting from large-scale development creates an issue of transfer: Which landowners will benefit and which landowners will lose out financially as the large landholding is developed? It is naïve to overlook the potential support for approval from those who will gain and the open disagreement from those who may lose. Such divergence of interest tends to maximize conflict.

The concept of value transfer indicates that land development occurs over a period of time. As such, it shifts from a single observable event to a series of events forming a process. By viewing land development as a process, the effect of different actions on the evolution of controversy becomes more apparent.

Urban Land Development: The Process

The process of land conversion provides the backdrop for the evolution of controversy we are discussing here. It is surprising that this subject was recently described by a National Commission as being relatively little understood and that conventional wisdom about the conversion process must be re-examined prior to the creation of national policy or programs.[7] The magnitude of the process is substantial and certainly has an impact on urban expansion. Nearly two million acres of land were converted from rural to nonagricultural special uses between 1950 and 1960 and a similar amount between 1960 and 1970. Of this total, over one-quarter consisted of direct additions to urban places and reflected the increasing geographic spread or fringe extension of most metropolitan areas.

Difficulty in gaining a clear understanding of the land-conversion process is attributed to its complexity and diversity. Incredibly fragmented and diffused among a wide variety and large number of private individuals and organizations and among many public agencies at each of the major levels of government, its complexity contributes to the opportunity for community controversy over a proposed development. There are many steps to the process, and interruptions in the sequence can disrupt or terminate a development. Different views of the process identify the various critical points at which controversy can prevent a development proposal from achieving its original objectives.

The main activities essential to real estate development as performed by the developer are illustrated in Figure 2.1.

1. *Need Determination.* Broad market evaluation to determine the need for and proper time for a proposed development.

2. *Site Evaluation.* Evaluation and selection of an appropriate location. (The often quoted three major principles of real estate development, in order of importance, are: (1) location; (2) location; and (3) location.)

3. *Site Analysis.* Determination of the principal features of a site for potential uses.

4. *Option/Purchase.* Arrangement for securing a location by ei-

7. National Academy of Sciences, *Urban Growth and Land Development: Report of the Land Use Committee of the Advisory Committee to the Department of Housing and Urban Development* (Washington D.C.: National Academy of Sciences, 1972).

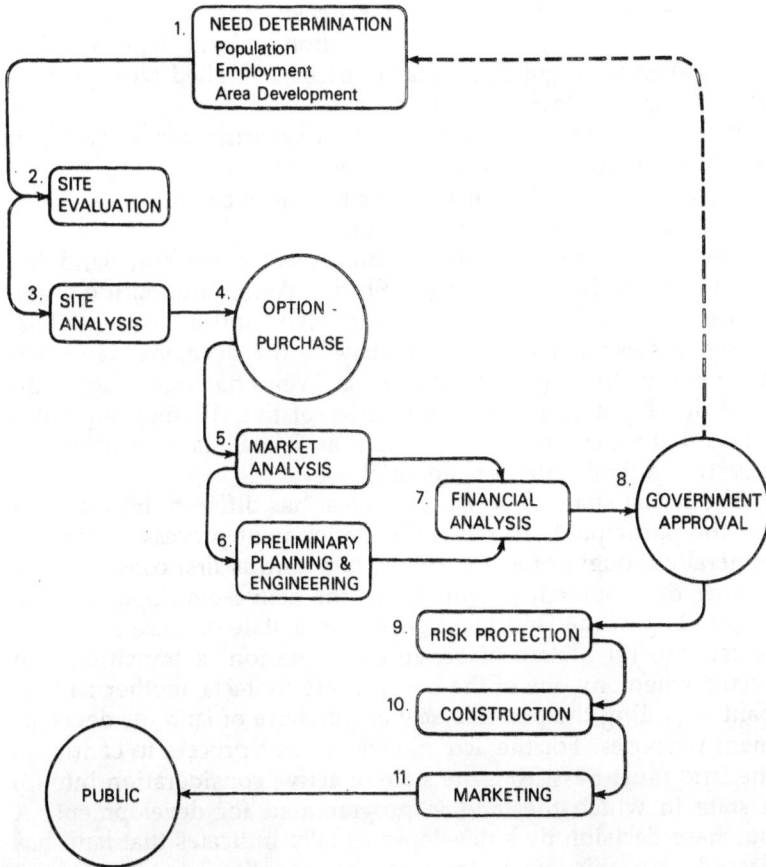

Figure 2.1. Real estate development process

ther option or purchase and the establishment of a method of financing.

5. *Market Analysis.* Preparation of surveys and analysis to provide the basis for a detailed physical layout and financial analysis.

6. *Preliminary Planning and Engineering.* Provision of detailed physical design of site for location of major facilities; and determination of relationships between public and private land users.

7. *Financial Analysis.* Preparation of projections for financial re-

turns, based upon cash flow, project costs, and project revenues.

8. *Government Approval.* Authorization by local, state, and federal bodies for regulations that must be complied with prior to starting project development.

9. *Risk Protection.* Arrangements for securing necessary insurances and bonds as protection against risks.

10. *Construction.* Installation of site improvements.

11. *Marketing.* Sale of improvements.

The real estate development process of converting land has been characterized according to Shirley Weiss and Marion Clawson by the small number of actors involved and its sequential nature.[8] In some cases the owner may be the developer, and perform many other tasks in the process. Weiss has conceived of the land-development process as a series of five discrete sequential states that move progressively from an initial state (or urban interest) to a final state of residential use.

The initial state (1) of urban interest has different implications for the participants in the land-development process. It may be generally thought of as the time when land is first considered as having development potential. For the active development process to begin, the land must pass from a state of mere urban interest into (2) a state of active consideration, a transition that occurs when any one of the participants contacts another participant regarding the possible sale or purchase of land for development purposes. For the active development process to continue, the land must pass from the state of active consideration into (3) a state in which the land is programmed for development. A purchase decision by a developer usually indicates that land has passed into this state. In many metropolitan areas of rapid growth the frequent turnover of land reflects more the importance of speculation in the local land market than the imminence of land development. Developers often withhold land for an in-

8. Some stimulating research on the development process has been done at the University of North Carolina. One report on the subject is the fourth in a series by Shirley F. Weiss, John E. Smith, Edward J. Kaiser, and Kenneth B. Kenney, *Residential Developer Decisions—A Focused View of the Urban Growth Process* (Chapel Hill: Center for Urban and Regional Studies, The University of North Carolina at Chapel Hill, 1966; reprinted 1974); Marion Clawson in *Suburban Land Conversion in the United States* (Baltimore, Md.: The Johns Hopkins University Press, 1971) described the decision-making process and the chief actors in urban expansion. See especially chaps. 5 and 6.

definite period of time for their own particular reasons. Until the land is purchased for a specific development purpose in a specific time period, the land remains in the initial state of urban interest.

For the process to continue further, the land must pass from the programmed state into (4) the state of active development, which is indicated by the filing of a development proposal with a governmental unit. Such a filing usually involves some commitment with regard to improvements on the land. For the active development process to end, the land must pass from the state of active consideration to (5) the state of actual conversion to an improvement. Upon marketing and purchase by a consumer, the land passes into this final state, and the urban land-development process is complete. In the aggregate, the development process involves a myriad of decisions among participants (or decision agents) including the landowner, the developer, and the consumer; supporting decision agents include realtors, financiers, and public officials.

Factors Influencing the Sequence of Decisions

Two factors that influence the outcome of key decisions in the land-development process are observed in urban renewal and transportation issues; these are (1) contextual environment; and (2) decision-agent characteristics.

Development decisions involve the cooperation of numerous parties, both public and private, who must participate in almost any venture. The sequence of decisions can be described as a "decision chain." The behavioral aspects of the land-conversion process relate to the independence of decisions. Because of this interdependence, and simultaneous dependence upon fact—technical standards; the appraisal of others regarding the relevant facts; and market, aesthetic, and other judgments—the decision-making chain is both complicated and at the same time highly dependent on custom or usage. None of the actors involved in these steps can act effectively unless most of the time reasonably accurate judgments are being made concerning the probable behavior of many other parties in the transaction. If the actors are frequently in error, they will shortly be out of business. If they propose anything radically new or different, they will be burdened with untold complications and the possibility of a turn-down by the municipality, other governmental agencies, the lender, the contractors, or ultimately the market. Such possibilities for failure obviously give a very conservative cast to all decisions made at every level and emphasize the interdependence of factors influencing decision-making.

1. *Contextual Environment*. Contextual factors provide the environment for developer decisions; these include the broad area-wide considerations that limit and determine the general type and amount of development. Two categories of contextual factors influence development: socioeconomic factors, and public policies. These factors provide the broad context for decisions, while at the same time they affect individual decisions in a direct manner. We have listed in Table 2.1 the contextual factors which seem important on the basis of available research.

Table 2.1. Contextual factors in development decision

Socioeconomic factors
  Geographic location
  Economic structure and growth prospects
  Community leadership
  Local housing market
  Local development industry
    Concentration
    Competition
  Psychology of the times
Public policy factors
  Federal policies
  State policies
  Local policies
    Investment and service
      Transportation
      Water and sewer
      Schools
      Community maintenance
    Regulatory
      Subdivision regulations
      Zoning
      Land use plan
      Annexation
    Tax

Source: Shirley F. Weiss, John E. Smith, Edward J. Kaiser, and Kenneth B. Kenney, *Residential Developer Decisions* (Chapel Hill: Center for Urban and Regional Studies, The University of North Carolina at Chapel Hill, 1966; reprinted 1974). Used with permission.

Public policies have four important dimensions which influence the development process: (a) the substantive provisions refer to the basic content of a policy, such as the cost provisions for the extension of water and sewer service; (b) the procedural provisions are often considered implicit, such as the petitioning and posting of bonds for extension of such services; (c) the flexibility of the policy refers to the extent of alteration of the provisions achieved through bargaining with public officials; (d) and the quantitative and general spatial distribution of policy refers to the proportion and general location of land in the area affected by the policy, such as all land within the city limits. Public policy as a contextual environment factor includes all four dimensions.

Socioeconomic factors and public policies provide such inputs to decisions as the following: limits on the direction and location of developable land in the metropolitan area (physical factors associated with geographic location); probable demand for new housing (economic structure, growth prospects, and local housing market); probable supply of new housing (the development industry); and general locations with development potential (local public policies). In addition, contextual factors determine such important considerations as the relative stability of the atmosphere in which development decisions are made.

Factors influencing the development process from outside the affected community should be considered in discussing the contextual environment. New communities are good illustrations of this point. The upstate New York areas do not exist in isolation from statewide and federal interests: decisions made in Albany, New York City, and Washington significantly affect the development process and, in turn, directly affect the local communities; statewide political interests are involved in the review of the proposals from many points of view; and federal interests are instrumental in the success or failure of the local proposal. From a broad perspective the goals and policies of state and national government on urban growth, support of housing and highways, and other social and economic programs influence actions at the local level. For these reasons a development proposal must be set within the context of varied levels of public policy.

2. *Decision-agent Characteristics.* (a) *Developer.* The four characteristics of the developer noted in Table 2.2 provide an explanation for much of the variation in behavior among developers.

Table 2.2. Characteristics of decision agents

Developer
  Type of firm
  Scale of operation
  Entrepreneurial approach
  Life cycle of firm
Landowner
  Place of residence
  Type of landowner
  Socioeconomic position
  Reason for holding land
Public officials
  Level of government
  Techniques for control
  Statutory and nonstatutory responsibilities
  Elected and nonelected officials
Consumer

Source: Shirley F. Weiss, John E. Smith, Edward J. Kaiser, and Kenneth B. Kenney, *Residential Developer Decisions* (Chapel Hill: Center for Urban and Regional Studies, The University of North Carolina at Chapel Hill, 1966; reprinted 1974). Used with permission.

"Type of firm" refers primarily to the extent of diversification, if any, of the firm's activity in residential and commercial and industrial development. "Scale of operation" refers to the annual production of housing units, regardless of the type of firm. "Entrepreneurial approach" refers to the broad personal attitudes that influence the manner in which developers make decisions, such as the developers' attitudes toward innovation in type of housing, risk in general, and scientific management. "Life cycle" of the firm refers to whether or not the entrepreneur and/or firm are newcomers in the development industry, or are developers with years of experience and reputation. The sophistication of a developer's approach varies within these four characteristics. The rueful comment of Weiss and her colleagues, after making a number of studies on the process, is significant in this connection:

Land development is obviously much more an ad hoc process than we had previously supposed. The unsystematic manner in which developers approach the production of residential lots indicates that most of the decisions made at this stage in the development process are probably made on the basis of their own experience, and a general awareness of "what's going on" in the local development industry rather than on the basis of what new techniques and ideas are available.[9]

Her comments are accurate for a vast number of development projects. They do not, however, reflect recent innovations in the requirements for analyses that are now included in applications for new-community financial assistance.[10] Accurate projections of cash flows for multimillion-dollar investments over a twenty- to thirty-year period have seen the introduction of refined analytical techniques into the urban land-development field.

(b) *Landowner Characteristics.* Predevelopment landowner characteristics are important because the landowner participates actively both in the decision to consider land for development and to sell land (the purchase decision). The ambivalent nature of the landowner in the development process can fluctuate from protagonist to antagonist. Predictability of this behavior is of interest to several participants in the process and is interactive with the physical, locational, and institutional characteristics of the property. By his transfer of ownership the landowner can generate community controversy and public policy. So, also, is public policy interdependent with land transfer as a causative factor in a landowner's actions and attitudes. The most influential element of local policy on the transfer of landownership is taxation. Predevelopment landowner attitudes toward holding or selling land are also related to changes in the use of land that is in close geographic proximity. Least likely to sell are those living on the land, those who are not retired, those who own the land singly, and those who have held the land longer than ten years but less than forty years. Most likely to sell are absentee owners, along with owners who are retired, who own the land jointly, or who have had their land either for a very short time or a very long

9. Shirley F. Weiss, Raymond J. Bugsby, and Newton W. Andrews, "Lake-oriented Residential Subdivisions in North Carolina: Decision Factors and Policy Implications for Urban Growth Patterns" *Research Previews* (Chapel Hill: Institute for Research in Social Science, The University of North Carolina at Chapel Hill, November, 1967), p. 13.

10. HUD new community submittals requirements are found in *Code of Federal Regulations*, Part 32, Title 24, July 31, 1971. An analysis of the requirements and a review of several financial models are summarized in Hugh Mields, Jr., *Federally Assisted New Communities* (Washington, D.C.: Urban Land Institute, 1973).

time. These factors have an important bearing on the actions of new-community developers as we will see later.

(c) *Public Officials.* The influence of public officials on the land-development process has been the subject of extensive investigation by political scientists in several case studies.[11] The empirical evidence of Edward Banfield examining Chicago, Harold Kaplan in Newark, and Clarence T. Davies in New York, supported earlier studies of political power by Banfield and James Wilson, Robert A. Dahl, and Floyd Hunter. A detailed analysis of the behavioral characteristics of public officials and their effect on policy at the local level must be expanded to other (and higher) levels of government as the scale of development is enlarged. For example, the influence of state and federal government on land development is becoming increasingly significant.

The growing literature covering political decision-making by local governments gives us some insight into the competence of these units to make development decisions affecting the metropolitan area. Local elected officials are predominately part-time public servants, involved primarily in their private business activities, and with little expertise in government. In addition, they tend to be people who are local in origin, rooted deeply in the traditions and economic circumstances of the past. These characteristics in some respects have poorly equipped them for the vastly different decisions of the present. When the Levitt concern moved into Falls Township in Bucks County, Pennsylvania, with its proposal to build a city of 15,000 homes, the township was governed by a group of local farmers whose total governmental experience in the preceding decades had involved decisions on the building of a small culvert, a short strip of country road, the addition of a wing to a school, and the like. Yet these were the people in charge of government for an area in which were to be built 300 miles of streets, sewers, and water lines, and $500 mil-

11. For example: Edward Banfield, *Political Influence* (New York: The Free Press, 1962); Harold Kaplan, *Urban Renewal Politics* (New York: Columbia University Press, 1963); Clarence T. Davies, *Neighborhood Groups in Urban Renewal* (New York: Columbia University Press, 1966); Edward Banfield and James Wilson, *Politics, Planning and the Public Interest—The Case of Public Housing in Chicago* (New York: The Free Press, 1955); Robert A. Dahl, *Who Governs? Democracy and Power in an American City* (New Haven: Yale University Press, 1961); and Floyd Hunter, *Community Power Structure* (Chapel Hill: University of North Carolina Press, 1953).

lion dollars' worth of public and private buildings. James Rouse and members of his staff have pointed out similar conditions in the development of Columbia, Maryland.

Studies of the behavior of political leaders in local government suggest that such people are strongly opposed to making decisions that involve conflict within the community. Case after case analyzing local development decisions reveal public officials as: (1) seeking to avoid tough decisions; (2) declining to confront issues before it is absolutely necessary to confront them; and (3), where decisions must be made, deferring to "experts" or to other levels of government, or delegating responsibility to nongovernmental groups which, it is hoped, can reach some sort of consensus. Local government is particularly sensitive to pressures from local groups. Since development decisions often involve threats— either to the property rights of some residents or, more dangerously, to their image of the community in which they live—any decision is likely to evoke the most impassioned responses from directly affected factions of the population. Local elected officials are poorly equipped to respond to these pressures. They must necessarily value the current applied pressures more highly than the less specific sentiments of the rest of the public or the long-run needs of the community. Their very tenure in office depends upon such an evaluation. Only within narrow limits do they have the opportunity or the power to delegate decision-making to others less vulnerable to local particularisms and short-term concerns.

As a consequence of these characteristics of the public decision-making process, large numbers of urgently needed decisions are put off indefinitely. Major highway decisions in almost every metropolitan area may take as long as ten years to resolve where local groups come into conflict with local, county, or state highway officials in controversies about the alignment of such facilities. The acquisition of sites for future schools and parks is frequently deferred until it is too late to buy the sites at reasonable prices. Zoning and subdivision control tend to be manipulated to preserve the past image of a rural community even when it is in the process of rapid conversion to a densely developed urban area.

Four methods of resolving local development controversies appear to be prevalent. (1) In a few instances local political leaders develop convictions about what is to the best interest of the community. They lay their political fortunes on the line and, as often as not, are defeated in the next election if they seriously attempt to stand up for what they regard as the community welfare. Such cases are rare, but frequent enough to induce a broad measure of caution in other elected officials. (2) Another approach is for the local officials to defer to the judgment of technical experts or higher levels of government. Particularly in the case of highway decisions, local officials take the position that the need for a highway or the need for a certain alignment is a technical matter, and say the engineers have settled it. Or they may say, "It is for the state to decide," or the state and the federal government, and "We cannot interfere with the decision." Occasionally, local officials will initially accept responsibility for a decision. Later, when the heat gets too great, they will defer to the technical character or the superior level of government responsible for the decision. (3) In a third approach, local officials seek to achieve consensus by referring decisions to citizen groups and organizations in a position to reach an accommodation, at least among activists. Here the technique is to appoint a representative citizen group which has some built-in reflection of the community tensions, but which is loaded in favor of what appears to be the least dangerous solution. Such committees are made responsible for reconciling conflicts within the community, developing an accommodation that will minimize antagonisms within the community, and suppressing or appeasing the opposition. When the group has come up with its compromise, public officials ratify and enforce it. (4) A fourth approach is to avoid ever making a decision. Deciding is postponed indefinitely, or until mounting demands for action force a solution through one of the mechanisms described above.

In larger government units very similar processes prevail. Even the largest cities have had considerable difficulty in making decisions regarding the alignment of expressways, the location of public housing projects, the location and character of urban renewal projects, the development of new shopping centers, and the adoption of modern zoning ordinances. Studies of decision-making in larger cities suggest that here, too, mayors are rarely willing to risk their political future to reach a decision which they may recognize as necessary for the public welfare. More commonly they will make all decisions that do not involve controversy, and seek to avoid making, or to avoid responsibility for making, decisions that involve controversy regarding the future of the area. In such larger cities the use of civic groups to reconcile conflicting pressures and to achieve accommodations is almost universal, and postponement for months and often years—occasionally decades—is common. Philadelphia, for example, has debated the alignment of the Delaware Expressway for more than a decade. New York has debated the expressway across downtown Manhattan for about thirty years. The costs of these delays are not easy to calculate precisely, but they certainly are enormous.

(d) *Consumer Characteristics.* The characteristics of the consumer as decision agent are important not only because the consumer participates in the purchase decision, but also because the developer bases his decisions on his perception of consumer preferences. The role of the consumer may be considered negligible as an element in community controversy in the urban land-development process, although the introduction of advocates for future residents of a development proposal at an early stage can sometimes offset the emergence of controversy.

Interaction of Participants in the Process [12]

Having described the characteristics of the various agents involved in the decision-making process for land development, we will briefly examine the interaction of the participants. To simplify the discussions, four broad categories of actors are used in the following discussion.

Although the obvious stage on which the actors perform their role is one which deals with local interests, influences from outside the local area are also effective. An issue of local interest can have statewide, national, or even international impact. Issues like those related to resource development and energy shortages, such as strip coal mining or oil refinery port locations, extend local concerns into a much broader arena. The roles of participants interacting in the new communities in our examples from

12. Roles of participants have been described by Clawson, *Suburban Land Conversion,* and other authors. However, Clawson introduces the interactions between actors in the process from initiation of a land-development proposal to marketing of the improvement. See pp. 101–109.

New York State have to be seen not as isolated local events but as part of an ambitious program for a national urban policy.

Figure 2.2 illustrates the four major actors and the interactions among and between them. First is the primary source that initiates the process: the landowner or the speculator. (These may also be people who own land but do not intend to develop it themselves.) Second is the considerable category of private businesses, all operating in search of a profit, each performing some function in the process of converting raw land into development. Nonelected public officials and public employees who are not selected by the voters but are appointed form a third category of groups involved in the process. (These officials include members of advisory boards or commissions mandated by statutory provisions, and employees of various public agencies with professional standards and criteria as well as professional expertise.) The fourth category includes the elected public officials.

These various interacting groups take raw land, financial resources, and construction expertise, and produce a commodity that is a component of the urban land-development process. The number of actors and their interactions expands proportionately with the complexity of a project. An opportunity exists in the development of new communities to examine a wide array of participants and determinants of interaction where this large-scale complex form of land development can be seen as a source for identifying factors significant to the successful acceptance of a proposed development scheme.

1. *Landowners, Speculators, and Dealers.* The central figures in the land-development process—the landowner, speculator, and dealer—work with a fixed commodity, the land. The greatest asset of this group is not land itself, but information.[13] These people seek to be well-informed about the status of public projects—both adopted and proposed plans. Also they want to know about exchanges of property and prices paid, which developers are involved, and what may be the demands for land in the very immediate future, and by whom and for what. The speculator profits primarily by his superior knowledge and his ability to take advantage of that knowledge.

Interaction between landowners or speculators, and categories

13. Clawson, *Suburban Land Conversion*, p. 101.

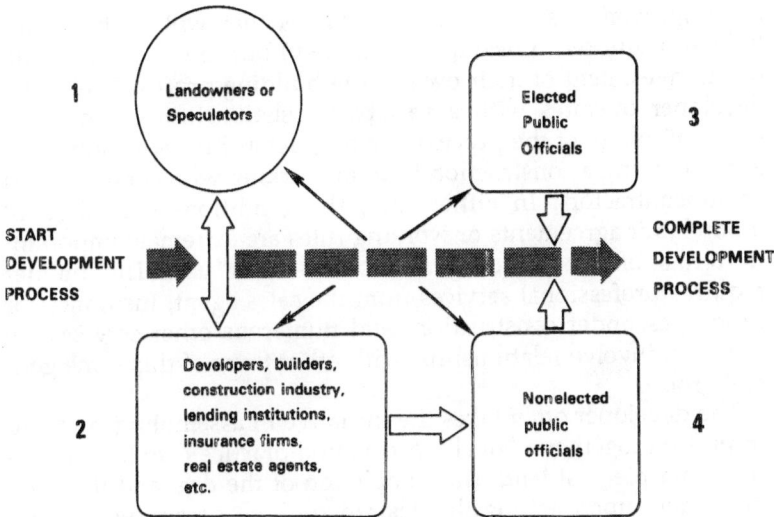

Figure 2.2. Interactions among participants in the land-development process

of the public sector, is influenced by the effect of public services on the value of land. Studies conducted for the Douglas Commission provide data supportive of the great influence that public policy, in installation of facilities and zoning of land, can have on the price of land.[14] The research clearly shows that in the course of transformation of land from rural to urban use, enormous values are created which encourage speculative activities that reinforce the tendency toward higher prices.

2. *Developer and Other Profit-motivated Participants.* Profit-motivated participants are distinguished from the landowners and speculators in that the developers, builders, and others in this group hope to make their profit from action rather than information and from the passage of time.

For example, the builders' operations are highly dependent upon sources of borrowed funds. Builders expect not only to sell

14. National Commission on Urban Problems (Douglas Commission). Several studies of the Commission bear directly on this question: Research Report no. 2: *Problems of Zoning and Land-Use Regulation; Research Report no. 11: Zoning Controversies in the Suburbs: Three Case Studies;* Research Reports nos. 12, 13, and 15: *Alternatives to Urban Sprawl: Legal Guidelines to Governmental Action* (Washington, D.C., 1968).

the improvements they build (at prices that will enable them fully and quickly to recoup their money) but to do so with little or no investment of their own in the building process itself. The developer operates with a variety of relationships in the construction phase of the process. He may act as his own contractor, either owning a construction firm, or working with combinations of subcontractors. In either case, the conditions embodied in union labor agreements or working rules are extremely important in terms of the building methods he can use. The builder requires professional services from the sales agent, insurance for properties under construction, and numerous other services, all of which involve relationships with other firms of this same general group.

The developer often takes the initiative in assembling land and in putting together a "deal." A common practice is to take an option on a piece of land, the completion of the deal and the price dependent upon getting the desired zoning or rezoning, assuming that the land is not already zoned as desired. This promptly brings the developer and/or the landowner into contact, first, with the nonelected professional staff of the zoning authority, then with the zoning board if the latter has appeal power over the zoning board. Equally important are the public services available to the tract of land in question, and this brings the developer and/or the landowner to the sewer authority, the water authority, the highway authority, and others. In each case, the developer seeks public actions which he believes are in accord with the rules governing such actions, but he often may have to persuade the public officials that what he wants is in fact in accord with such rules.

Of less immediate but perhaps of greater long-range importance are the relations between builders and those units of local government that establish building, safety, and health codes. These matters are less immediate because ordinarily they cannot be changed for a single subdivision, but more importantly because they set limits on where and what a builder can build. Building codes are widely attacked as unnecessarily restrictive and backward-looking, as inhibiting new methods of construction; but they are a tool the public can use to prevent dangerous or shoddy construction. The introduction of demanding environmental protection ordinances, which are rigidly enforced, has contributed to a slowing down of suburban construction. Enforcement has caused sharp contrasts between subdivisions and individual properties developed under environmental protection ordinances and those developed under lax enforcement of earlier land-use and building ordinances.

The developer-builder group utilizes lawyers to a major extent, particularly in zoning and rezoning cases, but also for help in preparing agreements and carrying out negotiations. Lawyers often play a critical role in such cases because of special knowledge, special bargaining skills, or possibly because of special influence with public officials. Conflicts of interest arise frequently where an area is dominated by one or several law firms. This is a phase of the suburban building process about which there is much concern and occasional evidence of illegal actions.

3. *Elected Public Officials*. Local government jurisdictions at the village, town, city, and county level have an elected governing board with general governing powers (the name of the board varies in different parts of the country). Such boards have mandatory control over the actions of the nonelected officials, including appointed boards and public employees.

The general governing board should set policies and develop consistent programs to carry out policies. In practice, the general governing body may be quite unable to exercise these broad powers. The board may be so smothered in detail passed up to them by their employees, or so captive to special political groups, within their city or county, or so incapable of controlling various specialized nonelective boards and commissions, that in fact they are able to exercise very little power. Often the members of the general governing group are themselves the representatives of special interest groups, and their real function is to prevent any public action inimical to the group they really represent.

Elected public officials, obviously overburdened in relation to their income and expected to appear frequently at evening meetings, are subjected to a variety of competitive pressures in performance of their office. Given all the undesirable aspects of public office, it is worth asking why men and women seek such offices—and nearly always in numbers that produce real competition for the offices. Various alternative explanations are possible: [15]

15. Clawson, *Suburban Land Conversion*, p. 106.

(a) Some persons are undoubtedly public-spirited, anxious to obtain good government for their city or county, and convinced (often rightly) that they can contribute to that end. Such individuals are members of informal groups, or of other more formal groups with similar objectives, that urge them to run for office and offer support. In a general skepticism over local governing bodies, one should not underestimate the power and motivation of such groups.

(b) Holding office on the local governing body may be a stepping-stone to a higher, better-paid, more prestigious public office, possibly in the state or federal legislature. In many areas of the United States, there is a considerable tradition of progressive public service, from local to state to national office, and service on a local governmental body may thus be considered a capital investment for a political future.

(c) The payoff may be direct, in actual cash in extreme cases, but more commonly in terms of better business deals for themselves or their associates. This sort of thing is suspected, gossiped about, or actually charged in political campaigns, in newspapers, and elsewhere. Only occasionally are formal charges brought, and these do not always result in convictions. One may assume that illegal acts are much less common than those legal acts where the result may be an equal betrayal of the general public interest. There are undoubtedly many legal ways to help one's friends; it is here that lawyers can provide valuable services.[16]

One major interrelation between the builder-developer group and the elected public officials arises at this point. A builder-developer, or the lawyer serving such businesses, may find it worth his while to seek public office and to devote to the affairs of the public body the time it requires; the direct financial gain to himself and his interests may fully repay any time and effort ostensibly devoted to the public business. In many suburbanizing counties, participation in the public political process usually comes from those who expect some direct financial gain from so doing. Officials in such counties are often landowners, anxious to sell at the best price, or builder-developers anxious to build with

16. This material was written prior to the scandals of the Nixon administration, including those involving the vice president and Watergate.

minimum public restrictions and with maximum public help, or they are lawyers or other agents of these groups.

4. *Nonelected Public Officials and Public Employees.* The non-elected public officials must be divided into two quite different groups: those who are members of appointed boards of various kinds; and those who are employees of the general and specialized local government agencies.

Throughout the United States, use is made of the appointed board—sometimes advising, often actually governing or operative. There are highway commissions, school boards, zoning commissions, planning boards, park and recreation boards, environmental quality boards, and many others at state, county, and local levels. Members of such boards may receive a small salary but only after their expenses are paid. Many boards are innocuous—their origins lie in tradition or they serve merely to provide a degree of public recognition to outstanding private citizens. However, in other instances such boards have real governing power and exercise it. The best defense for such boards is that the members serve overlapping terms which provide continuity, stability, and some measure of protection against irresponsibility. Some at times seem almost out of control of the general elective governing body.

Several such boards, for example, school, zoning, and planning, become the focus of attention in controversies over land development. In those issues in which public referendums are not the source of decisions, nonelected public officials and public employees create policy, and in so doing they act as surrogates for public opinion.

The employees of public agencies include professional staff and consultant architects, engineers, landscape architects, traffic engineers, economists, and others. In each instance it may be assumed that their basic desire is to perform their professional function as they define it, earn a good income, and to occupy a respectable place in the social hierarchy of the community. Each is conditioned by the nature of his professional training.

The planners, by virtue of education and experience, are employed to recommend policies for sound urban and land-use planning. Richard Babcock has described some of the problems of the planner: "The intolerable position of the planner is underscored by his suspicions that the final decisions will not be his."[17] The planner is constantly caught in a struggle between what he thinks is best from a broad social viewpoint and what he thinks the community—and more specifically the planning and/or zoning board—will accept. In a great many situations, the planner or zoning employee is under considerable pressure to give in to some individual or group that wants some public action to its particular profit. In such situations, the planning or zoning employee often has no political ally and only political opposition—it is no wonder that he loses so many such contests.

In any case, it is evident that the salaried employees of the public agencies in a suburbanizing county or city have numerous contacts with the elected public officials, with nonelected officials, with individuals in the private developer-builder industry, and with the landowner-speculator group. The salaried employee normally has limited political strength, but his knowledge and his position in the governmental process nevertheless nearly always make him a useful and sometimes a vital part of the whole process.

Summary

Opportunities for community conflict over urban land development exist as a result of the complex, interactive forces in an urbanizing society. As the United States has moved from a rural to an urban society, the physical pattern of the nation has changed drastically. Along with urbanization there has arrived a set of development patterns that are negatively described as sprawl. The consumption of land on the periphery of existing urban centers and the concomitant decay and abandonment of the central city is accompanied by suburbanization.

An antiurban philosophy has supported the opponents of urban land development and counsels the antagonists in emerging community conflicts. Implicit in some disputes over changes in the physical patterns of land use is conflict in the relationships between government and individuals. Social attitudes toward private rights and privileges in the American society are derived from constitutional doctrines such as due process, equal protection, delegation of legislative power, and the finality of adminis-

17. Richard F. Babcock, *The Zoning Game—Municipal Practices and Politics* (Madison: University of Wisconsin Press, 1966), p. 65.

trative decisions. Disparity of objectives is a contributing factor in the formation of opposition to a development proposal, and some adjustment of the developers' goals and those of society must be made to reach a point of mutual agreement to avoid community conflict.

The process of land development is an intricate sequence of events subject to a variety of pressures and constraints. Not to be overlooked are the larger state and national issues involved in the development process. This broadens the theoretical and empirical relevance of our community case studies. Since local communities do not exist in isolation from statewide and federal levels, they are affected by changes in the enabling legislation, financial appropriations, and condition of the state and national economy in the early 1970's. The case studies of new communities in the following three chapters and the local responses to the development proposals provide opportunities to look at the broad principles that can emerge about the development process.

3 | Lysander (Radisson)

By the end of 1973, three years after the passage of the Housing and Urban Development Act of 1970, fifteen new communities had been approved for federal guarantee under Title VII by the U.S. Department of Housing and Urban Development (HUD). Lysander New Community was unique among this group for several reasons: the project was sponsored by a public agency and not a private developer; federal grant assistance was sought, rather than guarantees for land acquisition and development; and the site was acquired by purchase from a single source.

Radisson (the name was changed from Lysander New Community in late 1973) provides the data for our first case study. Its short history is intertwined with the New York State Urban Development Corporation (UDC). We will diverge occasionally in this chapter to explain UDC, its background, and its activities, as a necessary component in understanding the emergence of controversy surrounding a proposal sponsored by a public agency. UDC developed two other new communities in New York State along with Lysander; Audubon near Buffalo, and Roosevelt Island (formerly Welfare Island, off Manhattan in the East River).

The acquisition of Lysander in the form of purchase in fee simple from a single source is an important fact in our discussion. By avoiding the subterfuges usually performed by large-scale land developers, UDC immediately by-passed the animosities and jealousies that occur with acquisition of individual parcels of land.[1] With no disgruntled neighbors to question what was going on with nearby properties, an early source of conflict in land assembly was avoided. Lysander was decided upon rapidly because initial investigations made it appealing for new-community development: it was a large undeveloped tract on the periphery of a metropolitan area, with a dynamically expanding economy, and with natural site characteristics amenable to low site-development costs.[2] With the resources of the State of New York committed to the project, some problems of the private developer could be overcome. However, the attitude of conservative upstate New Yorkers toward big government introduced a set of obstacles which were not faced by other Title VII new communities. Consequently, this experience of the New York State agency can be the reference for comparison purposes when questions arise over the involvement of government as a sponsor or participant in some major role in new-community development.

Project Description

Lysander New Community is located twelve miles northwest of the city of Syracuse. The site of approximately 2,700 acres is in Onondaga County, part of a three-county Standard Metropolitan Statistical Area (SMSA) of about 700,000 persons (see Figure 3.1). The development plan for a twenty-year period is to house a population of 18,000 persons in 5,000 housing units, to create jobs for 12,000 persons, and to provide a full range of community facilities.[3]

The principal goal of the UDC in undertaking the development of Lysander is described as the creation of an attractive balanced new community. The specific objectives of the development are:

1. See Edward P. Eichler and Marshall Kaplan, *The Community Builders* (Berkeley, Calif.: University of California Press, 1967), pp. 1–10. Also, for a description of James Rouse's activity in assembling Columbia, Maryland, see Gurney Breckenfeld, *Columbia and the New Cities* (New York: Ives Washburn, 1971), pp. 224–238.

2. These characteristics are described as "new-community development opportunities" in Advisory Commission on Intergovernmental Relations (ACIR), *Urban and Rural America: Policies for Future Growth* (Washington, D.C., April, 1968), pp. 98–103.

3. For a detailed description of the project and its requirements for compliance with federal and state regulations, see New York State Urban Development Corporation, *The New Community of Lysander, Onondaga County, New York: Final*.

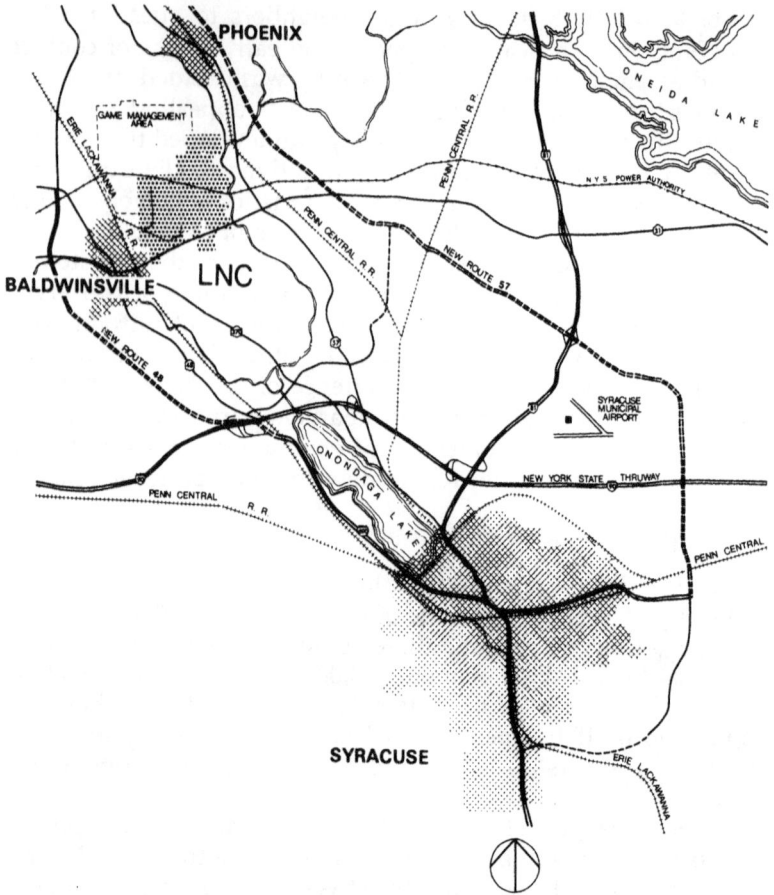

Figure 3.1. Map of Lysander New Community (LNC) and environs

1. To develop the greatest possible variety of types and sizes of housing to accommodate a full range of income groups, family types, and age groups.

2. To attract and retain industry in sufficient quantity and diversity to provide an adequate employment and tax base for the New Community and the surrounding area.

3. To develop public education facilities of the highest quality to meet the needs of both the New Community and the Baldwinsville Central School District.

4. To develop a high degree of public services needed by residents which can be supported by a tax base within the New Community sufficient at each stage of development so that the tax rates of existing jurisdictions are not adversely affected.

5. To develop the New Community in a way which respects and enhances the ecology and natural beauty of the area, especially in relation to the adjacent Three Rivers Game Management Area and the Seneca River.

6. To provide sufficient open space and extensive recreational opportunities for those living and working in the area.

7. To create, through quality architectural design, a harmonious physical environment while preserving opportunities for individual architectural expression.

8. To foster the orderly growth of the new community area by eliminating blighting influences, unsanitary conditions, and other negative characteristics which have tended to prevent or hinder the sound, orderly development of this site; and consequently, have adversely affected the natural growth of the Town of Lysander and the Syracuse Metropolitan Area.

9. To create sound development opportunities that will attract maximum private investment of capital and enable private enterprise to participate to the fullest extent possible in the implementation of the Plan.[4]

The history of the site and its relation to local government influence the emergence of controversy. Land used for farming in this part of the town of Lysander is held in differing sizes of parcels ranging from several to hundreds of acres. The assembly of the new-community site in a single landholding occurred at the beginning of World War II. Selected by the federal government as a site for manufacturing explosives, over 7,000 acres were purchased, 250 resident families evacuated, and a plant put into operation. The property was declared surplus after the war and some of the land was repurchased by the original owners. At this point events occurred which created the attractiveness of the parcel for speculation. The eastern boundary is formed by the Seneca River, an attractive natural limit to development. The State of New York purchased almost 3,000 acres of the north and west portions of the property for a Game Management Preserve. In 1947, a private developer bought 2,030 acres for a large housing development. The development did not materialize, and, in 1952,

4. New York State Urban Development Corporation, *Lysander New Community—General Project Plan*, April 1, 1971, pp. 3–4.

the land was bought by the William Waldorf Astor estate, giving the site its local name of the Astor Tract. Later, additional land was purchased, bringing the tract to 2,476 acres. The Astor estate did nothing with the land, and in 1968 the parcel was sold to a group of Syracuse businessmen for speculative purposes. It was brought to the attention of the UDC in July, 1968, by the Onondaga Industrial Commission, an arm of the Chamber of Commerce, and the Metropolitan Development Association, a private nonprofit corporation in operation since 1959. After several meetings with local representatives, UDC purchased the site in June, 1969.

To the southwest, the village of Baldwinsville is adjacent to the site. The village has had a stable population level of 6,000, and is divided between two rural towns, Lysander and Van Buren. Throughout its early history it has served as the traditional center for the surrounding rural area. Even though Baldwinsville lies in a major corridor of growth outward from Syracuse, the village has not been the focus of recent development in the area. Limited-access highways distributed development in the corridor, Main Street had deteriorated in appearance, and regional shopping centers were being considered to serve the residential subdivisions between Syracuse and the village.

As news spread of the state's proposal to build some kind of development adjacent to the village, concern over a community of unknown character three times as big as the existing center began to emerge. Local governments of the town, school district, and fire protection districts became anxious over the projected plans.

The northwest sector of Onondaga County was considered one of the fastest growing areas by the Onondaga County Planning Agency. Awareness of this trend and its effect on life styles raised fears among residents of Lysander and affected their attitudes toward future development. The Lysander proposal was set into this environment of concern.

Two other indicators of the region's potential for controversy can be found in political patterns and local crime rates. The politics of the area, typical of upstate New York, are conservative. The area consistently supports conservative fiscal management for state and local government and regularly returns slates of Republican candidates to local office. These are the politics which reluctantly supported the New York State Urban Development Corporation Act of 1968 and opposed measures of public intervention in matters of public welfare, housing, and urban development. Local crime rates are low in comparison to national rates by half and are 25 percent lower than in neighboring Rochester. These rates reflect local support for strong positions toward "law and order" and security for person and property. The community supports strong enforcement of the law, an attitude of considerable importance in suburban and rural areas. The need to preserve this status is strong in the minds of residents and mitigates against social change in the area.

The Urban Development Corporation Act permits development for various purposes, including residential use. The Act expressly defines residential projects as those "designed and intended for the purpose of producing housing accommodations for persons of low income." This portion of the Act has become the focus of resistance in the local community. The overall Lysander project is intended as a balanced new community. The final development plan must, by policy, include the housing mix, shown in Table 3.1.

UDC's mandate to provide a fixed percentage of low-income housing established an issue for community controversy. Ironically, UDC's provisions for upper-income housing also stirred controversy as a misuse of taxpayers' money.

Considerable effort by the Corporations' consultants, headed by David A. Crane, centered on market analysis and economic models. The economic consultant, Robert Gladstone and Associates, established realistic social, economic, and land-use data for

Table 3.1. Lysander housing mix: Dwelling units per income group

Income group	Number of dwelling units	Percent of total units	Population by group
Low income (elderly)	500	10%	700
Low income (other)	1,000	20%	3,249
Moderate income	1,000	20%	4,037
Middle income	1,250	25%	5,155
Upper income	1,250	25%	5,214
Total	5,000	100%	18,355

Source: Lysander Project Plan.

physical planning. Commercial development was limited by the practical constraints of the modest population envisioned for Lysander, as well as by the desire to gain support from the neighboring community of Baldwinsville by minimizing local merchants' fears. Prospective development in nearby suburban communities, coupled with regional shopping centers already in operation, influenced decisions against major commercial establishments at Lysander. The total area in the new community devoted to commercial facilities was designed primarily to serve the needs of the residents and was concentrated on approximately 25 acres of land in the town center and subcenter. Land allocated for purposes of industrial development was subject to negotiations between UDC and local government. Marketing of the allocated 800 acres was dependent on assistance from state agencies, while resident employment on the site was treated obliquely by the UDC. This was apparent in the UDC definition that the primary role of industrial development in the new community was to provide desirable, fully improved sites to private industry. Complete development of the industrial park is expected to provide up to 12,000 industrial jobs. A summary of land use at final development is shown in Table 3.2.

Two critical concerns expressed by the consultants during project planning were the UDC commitment to the site location and the projected population mix. The first of these dealt with the project's location outside the existing and projected development patterns within the Syracuse metropolitan area. The economists found the location of the site was not good in relation to existing

Table 3.2. Lysander land use

Land use	Acres	Percent of total
Residential	910	34.1%
Community facilities (including commercial)	168	6.3%
Open space	597	22.4%
Industrial development	795	29.8%
Land reserves	200	7.4%
Total	2,670	100.0%

Source: Lysander Project Plan.

development activities. State agency support would be necessary to promote development by locating new state-supported facilities in the community and by providing highway access. This point was made by local critics of the project familiar with the regional growth patterns in recent years. The second concern of the consultants involved the state's commitment to provide low-income housing. Probably the cause for the greatest local concern and resistance to the project was that the prospective population would be over one-quarter low-income households. The source of these households from outside the community and the possible racial mix caused early negative reactions among the local residents. The potential impact of these poverty families on local social services and schools, and UDC's inability to satisfy fears, caused distress among local residents. Ironically, Baldwinsville is one of the poorest villages in the upstate New York region as measured by income and public welfare support.

The Urban Development Corporation

Two aspects of the Lysander project provide special interest: the origins of the Urban Development Corporation and the assemblage of the site. Both actions are unique in new-community projects and deserve a brief description at this point. The uniqueness of UDC has provided controversy from inception and has been reported in both national and local media. This publicity was sustained at the announcement of the Lysander project and provided a future source for criticism by local opponents. The history of the site, its purchase, and the speculative aspects related to the sale of a large tract also generated opportunities for local critics of the project.

Announcement by Governor Nelson Rockefeller on February 27, 1968, of a state-sponsored corporation to rebuild slums should be placed in the context of the urban riots of 1967 and the observable failures of federal urban renewal.[5] As one of New York State's contributions to "creative federalism,"[6] the corporation was viewed as a new state initiative in urban affairs. Reaction to the governor's proposal was mixed, with strong negative

5. *New York Times*, Feb. 28, 1968.
6. William K. Reilly and S. T. Schulman, "The State Urban Development Corporation: New York's Innovation," *The Urban Lawyer*, 1:no.2 (Summer, 1969), 129–146.

comment coming from Mayor John Lindsay of New York City. The appointment of Edward T. Logue, formerly of the Boston Redevelopment Administration, as president of the corporation may have affected Lindsay's adverse opinion and his presentation of a rival plan.[7] (Logue had rejected a job offer from Lindsay in 1966—he no doubt had foreseen possible difficulties in his relations with New York City.) The public differences between Governor Rockefeller and Mayor Lindsay drew attention to the proposed legislation's most controversial aspect, the state's power over local governments. The *New York Times* editorialized that the bill would "leave the State as the plenary power to ride roughshod over local and regional plans and to ignore local sentiment."[8] As the date of annual closing for the New York State legislature approached in April, the final debate on the bill was upset by the assassination of Martin Luther King. Governor Rockefeller urged that the law be enacted as a memorial to the slain leader.

Mayor Lindsay and the *New York Times* agreed on opposition to the UDC bill, seeing in its new powers to over-ride city building and zoning codes a threat to municipal integrity and home rule.[9] Opposition, apparently from reform Democrats, arose because to them it appeared too much like other housing measures for the poor. Suburban legislators of the governor's own party fought the bill as an obvious aid to the state's larger cities, and as a bill carrying a potential danger of imposed housing integration outside of the cities. To upstate rural interests, it appeared to offer nothing and found little favor.

The bill passed on April 10, 1968. The *Times* accused the governor of exerting strong pressure and "arm twisting" to secure passage.[10] Rockefeller admitted that he would refuse to cooperate with dissenters in the signing of their favored bills or in making appointments, and at the same time emphasized his personal commitment to city rebuilding by strong support of Logue and the UDC in its early stages of organization. This support was sustained by the governor through various election-year challenges and state budget crises until in June, 1973, the legislature voted to limit some of UDC's powers. Now local government can

7. *New York Times*, March 7, 1968.   8. *Ibid.*, April 11, 1968.
9. Reilly and Schulman, "The State Urban Development Corporation," p. 131.
10. *New York Times*, April 11, 1968.

veto proposals, although UDC still has the power to condemn, clear land, and relocate displacees. The UDC is specifically exempted from municipal permit-granting powers and obtaining certificates of occupancy. Obligations to "work closely, consult and cooperate with local elected officials and community leaders, to give consideration to local and regional goals and policies as expressed in urban renewal, community renewal and local comprehensive land use plans and regional plans," [11] are hedged by specific prohibitions against mandatory modifications by municipalities of any UDC plans or drawings. [12] Most publicized of all the UDC bill provisions were those authorizing the UDC to waive local laws, ordinances, zoning codes, charters, and construction regulations, substituting compliance with New York State's own building construction code, "when, in the discretion of the Corporation . . . compliance is not feasible or practicable." [13]

Armed with this mandate, Logue invited proposals for projects from municipalities in the state. Considering local governments' frustrations with federal urban renewal, UDC offered an attractive force for redevelopment. The response was encouraging. One of the earliest projects brought to the attention of the UDC was the proposed new community at Lysander. Logue evidenced a character of restraint in his earliest months of administration. By acting only upon municipal invitations and concentrating on urban problems, he was able to allay the fears that critics expressed of an aggressive state bulldozer. Logue, however, was looking to the future. If the first phase of work was rebuilding slums, then the second phase would be concentrated upon vacant land in suburban communities, and the third phase would be the building of new communities. Because of the availability of an assembled block of land, UDC decided to move forward on a new community at Lysander as an early project.

In the fall of 1968, Logue asked his former associate from Boston, David A. Crane, then head of his own planning firm, to coordinate a design team to examine the feasibility of a new community in Lysander. Crane's findings recommended purchase of

11. New York State Urban Development Corporation Act. Quoted in *McKinney's Unconsolidated Law*, chap. 184, §7, Laws of 1968, §§6251–6285, as amended through June, 1971.
12. *Ibid.*   13. *Ibid.*

the site. Additional acreage was acquired to expand the site to approximately 2,700 acres. Although planning was conducted in great secrecy, local people became aware of the activity, and, by the time of publishing the UDC progress report in August, 1969, local sentiment had begun to develop against the project.

The earliest attacks on UDC were directed at the secrecy in which unknown plans were being formulated. Whispered accounts of millions of dollars exchanged by land speculators were not quieted by the confidential treatment of early planning stages. The physical presence of various consultants surveying, soil testing, and taking traffic counts confirmed rumors of development. Regular helicopter overflights and landings on the site offered announcement of daily activities to site neighbors.

The legislation creating the UDC states that it shall "work closely, consult, and cooperate with local elected officials and other community leaders" and "shall give primary consideration to local needs and desires and shall foster local initiative and participation in connection with the planning and development of its projects." [14] What steps was UDC taking to meet its requirements for cooperation with local municipalities?

In the early months of the project, UDC did nothing to incorporate existing community leadership into the development process. It was operating on an accelerated planning schedule. A deadline of fall, 1969, was arranged for a public hearing as prescribed by law.

Voices of Concern [15]

Lack of information, particularly during the beginning period of a development project, becomes a primary factor in creating antagonism in the community. At Lysander, local community leaders, either elected or from influential businesses or political positions, were not brought into the early planning stages, which were directed by a regional office of UDC in Rochester, headed by John Stainton. Stainton's office dealt mainly with representatives of local power and influence from the Metropolitan Devel-

14. *Ibid.*

15. Many of the "voices of concern" and opinions quoted in the remainder of this chapter were from members of the community and region and represent the local elite. Their comments were selected as presenting an informed and influential position.

opment Association in Syracuse, and seldom with the local leadership.

Opposition crystallized in January, 1969, with the formation of the Greater Baldwinsville Homeowners' and Civic Association (HOCA). The membership of two existing subdivision homeowners' associations from Candlewyck and Aneta Manor, which had been formed originally to represent homeowners in conflict with the tract developers and local government, joined together to express fears and concern about UDC's proposal for the Astor estate. When Chester Smith, recently defeated Van Buren town supervisor, was elected president of the new group, meetings were scheduled, dues established, and a newsletter proposed. Immediate focus was placed on finding out UDC's plans for the area and investigating UDC's authority and capability for a multipurpose project.

Early negative reaction to the project proposal prompted UDC to retain the Policy Institute of the Syracuse University Research Corporation (SURC) to study aspects of the project criteria. SURC's report, published in June, 1969,[16] described the citizens' group as well organized and vocal, but uncertain whether they represent the majority except with respect to "lack of information." In the spring of 1969, HOCA claimed a membership of 400, a number representing less than a third of the occupied homes in Lysander. SURC further noted at that time that in the absence of organized sentiment favoring the new community the opposition could seriously threaten the speed and ease of development, if not the ultimate outcome, of the project.

The Association's position was clearly stated in a paper issued by its board of directors after a meeting on March 24, 1969.[17] After explaining that their opposition was to an Urban Development Corporation project in Lysander rather than to the general concept of such a project, ten specific points of issue were offered:

1. The authority to over-ride local zoning destroys the work of the Lysander Planning Board and Lysander Town Board.
2. The authority to over-ride local objections denies residents of the

16. Syracuse University Research Corporation (SURC), *The Lysander New Community* (Syracuse, N.Y., June 15, 1969).
17. Board of Directors, Greater Baldwinsville Homeowners' and Civic Association, Inc. (HOCA) (Mimeographed; April 14, 1969).

community any real voice in the character of the community being affected.

3. The tax-exempt provision of the Urban Development Corporation law would deny Lysander the normal opportunity to broaden its real estate tax base for new industry.

4. Long-time pay-back guarantees by private developers are impossible.

5. The Urban Development Corporation Law concentrates too much power in the hands of a few men.

6. The law does not provide for the development of new communities, particularly out in a remote country location away from the principal city being served.

7. Subsidized housing is likely to start nearby neighborhoods on the road to becoming slums.

8. The special inducements which the Urban Development Corporation can offer to industry, combined with subsidized housing in Lysander, may accelerate the development of slums in Syracuse.

9. Conversion of land now zoned industrial to residential use is undesirable in Lysander in view of the abundance of other open land in the town that is desirable for residential development.

10. The Urban Development Corporation inducements to industry,to locate in Lysander will constitute discrimination against industrial zones in the Towns of Van Buren and Clay and in southern Oswego County.[18]

The board of directors stated that they had not taken a position opposing the plan because none had yet been proposed in complete detail. Their arguments were procedural and they opposed the UDC incorporation law, taking the position that the project exceeded the authority of the law.

HOCA's basic objectives were "to promote sound and progressive development of the Greater Baldwinsville area." In the opinion of one observer: "public meetings sponsored by this organization have been apathetic on issues not connected with cost or ghetto problems" (i.e., not agitated by political and legal questions). It appeared that local sentiment was generally against the new community because of a feeling of uncertainty about what was planned.[19]

Several of HOCA's objections referred to home rule and UDC's ability to ignore local objections and opinions. Reference was made to the efforts, from 1964 on, of the Lysander and Van Buren

18. HOCA, *Bylaws.*

19. The conclusion was reached in the report by SURC, *The Lysander New Community,* Vol. I, pp. II–7.

town boards in preparing master plans and zone ordinances. The preparation of these documents had developed local interest in the planning process and an awareness of the problems and benefits of urbanization and land-use controls. Thus, an environment for comprehensive planning had already been established in the local area. But the Lysander investment in time and money (a $5,000 share of local money in the $30,000 federal and state-aided "701" planning project) in the preparation of planning material—which was never used by the UDC—was later pointed to by the Association and the *Baldwinsville Messenger* as an illustration of UDC's disdain for local participation in the new-community project.

Adoption and publication of the HOCA resolution created a demand for confrontation with UDC. To the HOCA board of directors, this meant Edward Logue. On April 8, Logue, Stainton, Crane, and other participants in the project were present at a public meeting. A majority of those present were opposed to the new-community project, the UDC, and Logue. Later, however, Logue was characterized as "frank and forthright . . . a man of action, impatient with red tape, and inbred with a sense of urgency to get on with solving the problems of city slums . . . a human dynamo."[20] HOCA suggested that Logue needed the counseling of local homeowners and that he should give more than lip service to local ideas. A general observation of the meeting, as reported in the *Baldwinsville Messenger*, was that big, powerful government had arrived on the scene and was in motion.

Logue did not return to Baldwinsville until the public hearing of May 17, 1971.

Through the late spring and early summer of 1969, the project moved ahead. In June UDC purchased the major part of the 2,700 acre tract. In July, 1969, UDC opened a field office in Baldwinsville, where Irwin Davis, an employee assigned by the Metropolitan Development Association, began an intensive public relations campaign to disseminate information on the project. It became apparent to Davis as he spoke to various community and social groups, sometimes three a day, that HOCA represented a minority of the community. There were others—the people to

20. HOCA, April 14, 1969.

whom he spoke and the casual visitors to the office—who sincerely sought information about the project.

Davis later observed that "sentiment was generally against the new community because of a feeling of uncertainty about what was planned." This being the case, Davis concluded that "sentiment generally against" was equivalent to "undecided." His efforts were an important step in convincing the undecided residents.

An editorial in the *Syracuse Herald-Journal* of May 28, 1969, summarized local concerns:

Why are the Town of Lysander and Baldwinsville residents objecting? We can cite three reasons:

First, they feel left in the dark with little control over their destiny as altered by the promised development.

Next, they feel threatened by new taxes for expected schools and services expansions but they're not sure about this either.

Finally, they feel put upon by the plans for 20 percent of the projected rental housing to go to low income individuals and families . . . some of whom might be clients of the social services department.[21]

As the overall situation presented itself, there were four basic concerns: (1) lack of information; (2) loss of home rule; (3) probability of increased ownership costs; and (4) possibility of creation of a ghetto within their town. UDC had to develop a course of action that would clarify the opportunity for participation, resolve the allocation of costs, and remove the ghetto notion from consideration.

An unsettling feeling of dismay over the loss of a way of life was usually expressed by people Davis interviewed, most of whom appeared to be free from personal economic loss or racist attitudes. People who had freedom of choice for selection of place of residence either were native to the area or had opted for a small town or rural setting where they could be free of the social problems connected with urban areas. A future for the Baldwinsville area in which governmental action would affect personal choice was anathema to local residents. If the expressed preferences for small-town life styles or the fear of excessive tax burdens were public postures to divert attention from private feelings of racism, there was no data to support the possibility. That

21. *Syracuse Herald-Journal*, May 23, 1969.

a favorable climate did exist was shown by a local resident who commented when leaving a HOCA meeting:

I came from the meeting feeling that the Project was a feasible and positive approach to a growing Baldwinsville. I can see nothing but benefit to our community in the long run. The tax burden of the present community will be lightened by the incoming industry and there will be more homeowners contributing property taxes.

The whole question boils down to how we want Baldwinsville to grow. It is one of the last suburbs in the northern part of Onondaga County with room to grow and the completion of major highways to the east and west of Baldwinsville will bring a fairly large influx of people. Do we want uncontrolled growth as in North Syracuse, Mattydale, and Cicero, or do we want a planned development with restrictions and regulations that will benefit the present community.[22]

Davis was a native of Syracuse and aware of the conservative nature of upstate New Yorkers. From his office in Baldwinsville he went about the task of informing residents about the program and overcoming the resentment caused by earlier visits of UDC officials. Davis' job was to take the negative attitudes toward UDC and develop at least a noncommittal or undecided frame of mind within the community. Much of his labor revolved around getting more information about the project into the community and involving the community in the planning process, for without the direct involvement of the community leaders in the project the misconceptions would sustain the pattern for community controversy and evolve into conflict, as described by James Coleman in his book, *Community Conflict*.[23] The Syracuse University Research Corporation (SURC), hired by UDC to analyze policy questions in establishing the new community, summarized the initial issues.

The core issue, in the economic sense perhaps as fully as in the social sense, lies in the misconceptions about that portion of Lysander New Community housing which has been announced as "low income." There is widespread feeling that a financial burden will be imposed on the town to subsidize such housing and the people who will occupy it. There is a very strong sense that once the floodgates are opened, there will be no end to the spread of a ghetto throughout the Town. People see

22. Letters to Editor, *Baldwinsville Messenger*, May 8, 1969.
23. James S. Coleman, *Community Conflict* (New York: The Free Press, 1957), pp. 9–14.

retail markets as being depressed, schools as being degraded while taxes are increased, and a way of life destroyed.[24]

The SURC report counseled that the answer would not be found in countering such fears with the assurance that housing was also to be built in Syracuse. As the newspaper reported it, the townspeople were asking that low-income housing be built entirely in Syracuse. What needed to be attacked was the misconception itself. UDC had to make clear that low-income housing is a necessary and beneficial part of community planning.

A context for planning in the village of Baldwinsville and the town of Lysander was expressed in *A General Plan for the Development of the Town*, published in 1964. Ample evidence was available for the committed position of community leadership in the plan's emphasis on the need for public discussion and public control.

Priority in such a situation (i.e., where there are alternative programs) will be determined by the effectiveness of public discussion and may be reflected in the results of public referenda to authorize financing. [We can recognize] that priority determination rests finally with the electorate.[25]

This clear position on public discussion of issues was an indication that town residents would resist development proposals counter to those prepared five years earlier and which they had not participated in. SURC foresaw that resistance would come: "They, like every other public group at every social and economic level, are simply reserving to themselves the right to share in the decision-making process with respect to their community."

Community Advisory Committee

On August 7, 1969, the Urban Development Corporation took two major steps toward gaining community support for the project: first, the publication of a "Staff Progress Report" containing the preliminary results of development planning for the new community in the town of Lysander, and, second, the announcement of the appointment of fifteen citizens of the Baldwinsville-

24. SURC, *The Lysander New Community*, Vol. I, pp. II–9, 10.
25. *Ibid.*, pp. II–12. Quoting from *A General Plan for the Development of the Town* (Lysander, N.Y., 1964).

Lysander area to serve on the Community Advisory Committee (CAC).

The staff report, which followed UDC's purchase of the site in June, concluded that the proposed site was well suited for development of a new community and that the multipurpose project would sustain a variety of functions: residential, commercial, industrial, recreational, and other land uses. It was estimated that some $240 million would be invested in the community at full development with about $200 million of this as private investment. The report provided the first detailed information to the community on the project. Planning was described as in an early and formative stage. Requirements for review, public participation, and a statutory hearing were outlined. The report provided substance for a concerted public relations campaign to gain local acceptance of the project, a campaign in which emphasis would be placed on rational land development benefiting the local economy and the involvement of the community in future decision-making. Industrial development would be given prominence over residential to insure adequate local tax revenues to support necessary services. Public relations activities were stepped up at the Baldwinsville site office, where Davis' local background and his family's ownership of a nearby farm were pointed out. Local media received a continuous supply of material, with a special section on Lysander published in the August 25, 1969, *Baldwinsville Messenger*. However, the support and integration of local leadership into the planning process and the building of long-term credibility were to depend upon the Community Advisory Committee.

Creation of an advisory committee has become an inherent part of citizen participation in governmental matters. Although the letter of the charge to a committee indicates the tasks and promises of such a group, the background of the committee selections, and that of the committee members themselves, provides insight into the aims of the selecting body. A broadly representative group, representative, that is, of different economic interests and minority groups, implies a desire for broad-based involvement. The size of a group and its geographical representation is also an indication of the nature of community input. Altogether, though, the advisory function can be construed as not more than the name implies: advisory. In fact, the UDC Act describes local involvement as "review and advise." But as an instrument of governmental policy, the advisory committee can be a powerful ally by disseminating policy and gaining public support.

What is revealed by the origins and constituency of the Lysander New Community CAC? Members of the committee were selected by the Urban Development Corporation representative, the Metropolitan Development Association (MDA). Supported by the power elite of the region, MDA seeks to promote the economic interests of the area. Bankers, manufacturers, and major entrepreneurs are prominent in the membership. In other areas the MDA has been noticeably slack in activities to improve the social interests of the community's minorities. Selection of the Lysander Community Advisory Committee by the MDA involved also the assistance of the supervisor of the town of Lysander, the mayor of the village of Baldwinsville, and the chairman of the board and the superintendent of the Baldwinsville School District, the Baldwinsville Chamber of Commerce, the county legislator from the town of Lysander, and the Onondaga county executive. Appointments were also checked by State Senator John Hughes, senior local legislator to Albany and recognized as a leader in the fiscally conservative upstate New York area. The members of the Community Advisory Committee were regarded by the MDA as well-respected citizens, and included: Walter McCarthy, chairman, a retired industrialist formerly with Morris Machine Works; Richard Stafford, vice chairman, an executive for Carrier Corporation and former president of the Baldwinsville Jaycees; Raymond McCarthy, former mayor of the village of Baldwinsville; Harry Beebe, chairman of the town of Lysander planning board; Maurice E. Cox, Onondaga county legislator; Lynus Duger, vice president of the Seneca Federal Savings and Loan Association; Cecil E. Reeves, a member of the town of Lysander planning board; James B. Schneider, staff member of the Syracuse chamber of commerce; Jane Schiener, a member of the Baldwinsville library board; Arthur J. Hewitt, sheet and plate divisional controller of Alcan, Inc., and president of the Baldwinsville Central School District board of education; Walter P. Thompson, a real estate broker and member of the Lysander town board; Luella McNeill, executive secretary of the Greater Baldwinsville Chamber of Commerce, and Leslie Delaney, retired, currently a member of the Baldwinsville board of trustees. Duger was the only member of the Homeowners' Association appointed to the committee. Other than Duger, the committee members can be characterized as representative of the general sentiment of the area to the project: conservative in politics and socioeconomic matters.

The fact that committee members received $50 per day did not ingratiate the group with the community. CAC meetings were open to the public but were not heavily attended. HOCA officers recall having been requested to leave at different meetings, although this was only during executive sessions. A search of local newspaper files for the period from August, 1969, to the public hearing in 1971 does not reveal mention of any of CAC activities. The group did not take an activist role in raising public awareness of the project nor did it broaden community knowledge of the plan. It is claimed by the Homeowners' Association that what little criticism the CAC did make of UDC, after the public hearing, was based on material originally prepared by HOCA. The lack of activity by the CAC during the initial months of emerging public opinion toward the project tends to support this opinion. The committee neither ameliorated UDC's position nor exacerbated local sentiments toward the project. These roles were sustained respectively by Irwin Davis and the Homeowners' Association.

Several criticisms leveled at the CAC were that its organization was "too little, too late." It was criticized as being unaggressive. A lack of public exposure and a "low profile" for committee activities tend to confirm this point of view. Findings of the committee were not publicized in local media, nor did the committee become a public forum for the project. Baldwinsville is amply supplied with social, service, religious, and other organizations which can provide exposure for new-community programs. Church groups, PTA's and the Chamber of Commerce were approached by UDC and MDA through the media and personally by Davis. The Homeowners' Association also approached these groups. The CAC did not attempt to obtain local discussion of the project.

UDC's strategy became one of persuasiveness and dissemination of information leading toward the public hearing in the spring of 1971. The Homeowners' Association recognized it had a difficult task against UDC's and MDA's resources if it was to sustain the community's negative attitude, for an informed public was being created: in effect, Davis was overcoming the poor impressions created by UDC's earliest efforts. HOCA required public exposure and an invigorated position to broaden the resistance to the new community. Such an activity occurred in the publishing of a counterproposal for development of the Baldwinsville area by HOCA.

Strategy of Dissent

Publication of UDC's Staff Progress Report and continued frustrations at influencing the basic concept convinced the Homeowners' Association that it was not succeeding in blocking the project for the new community. Smith and the HOCA board of directors analyzed the various prospects held open to them and selected two areas of possible effectiveness. The first dealt with limited objectives, that is, the project per se; inevitability was accepted but a continuous effort could be made to modify goals and objectives that disturbed area residents. The second area of endeavor was to attack the constitutionality and the procedures of the Urban Development Corporation itself.

Many of the techniques used successfully by suburban and rural antagonists of subdivision proposals center on local governments' decisions on zoning variances. However, the extraordinary powers of UDC pre-empt this option from action by either local government or private citizens. Because of UDC's desire to achieve public cooperation and an image of restraint, the Homeowners' Association decided to take a public position of positive criticism. This opportunism could be construed as an acceptance of Logue's "invitation," offered in his *Annual Report* as president in 1969 and 1970. Logue had cautioned that UDC had been granted extraordinary powers by the state legislature but that it sought a partnership approach.

The purpose of UDC's broad statutory powers is sometimes misunderstood. We do not consider it to be a license to ride arbitrarily over the legitimate interests of others. Rather, we regard it as a deterrent against the unilateral application of narrow purposes which are contrary to the general public interest. It is, of course, an expeditious way to bypass obsolete systems and procedures which prevent the accomplishment of agreed-upon public objectives.

We have not had to invoke all of UDC's powers, but we have found them to be invaluable in fostering mutually beneficial negotiations. In all communities in which we are active, we have sought to establish a working partnership with local civic leaders, local public officials, local community residents and local developers. We have viewed our role as a catalytic one, doing things which are not easily done by established public or private enterprises.[26]

In order to test Logue's desire to listen to local opinion, the Homeowners' board of directors decided to respond to the UDC Staff Progress Report in a form conceived to increase community opposition to the project. Several groups were recognized as sources of organized dissent. One group was comprised of those residents immediately adjacent to the proposed project. Their fears were related directly to rumors that a low-income ghetto was to be built next to their homes. This prospect was elaborated on with visions of obnoxious industries also built on the site. A second group was made up of those residents of the town of Van Buren who were disgruntled that the new community was not going to be built in their town. A sense of boosterism and wounded pride emerged. Coupled with the loss of tax revenues was the disappointment of wasted efforts to attract industrial development to the town. Chester Smith was in the vanguard of this point of view. A third group, and probably the most difficult to rationalize, was the conservative element who often used arguments of invasion of private rights as a cloak for racism. Chester Smith and the Homeowners' board of directors proposed to crystallize these different factions into a group seeking positive means to incorporate UDC's potential benefits into the area. Ostensibly formulating strategy for a legal contest over UDC's legitimacy, HOCA set out to improve its public image by providing an alternative to the August, 1969, Staff Progress Report.

After several months of reviewing the UDC Staff Progress Report, the Homeowners' board of directors prepared A Proposed Total Community Plan for Greater Baldwinsville,[27] and circulated it to board members. The proposal was unanimously adopted by the board at its meeting of February 10, 1970, and by the membership at the March meeting. The main thrust of the plan was

26. UDC, Annual Report, 1969 and 1970.
27. HOCA, A Proposed Total Community Plan for Greater Baldwinsville, New York (Feb., 1970).

that since UDC had invited local participation, the community was acting responsibly by asking for a comprehensive approach to solving local problems. It suggested that existing population centers be strengthened and that development on the new-community site be limited to an industrial park and a residential neighborhood. The issue of home rule was emphasized by insistence on the planning procedure "encompassing the participation of local people and organization throughout the community, with final approval limited to the Lysander Planning Board."[28]

The board of directors organized their plan into four sections: (1) an introductory statement, (2) disadvantages of the UDC proposal, (3) suggested principles to guide sound development, and (4) a proposed plan. Concern was focused on UDC not having taken the people of the community into its confidence in the development process and on the inherent disadvantages of the new-community concept. HOCA suggested that although UDC's plan had many serious disadvantages, certain modifications in the plan would overcome their disadvantages. Claiming to have had a lengthy period for review of the UDC plan and a broad base of local and professional support in its contentions, the board proceeded to criticize the UDC report, item by item. HOCA's report put much emphasis on the need for public input from the community as a team effort. Two strong points in HOCA's favor were that the planning process had not been integrated with local government and that the UDC plan did not consider the economic impact of the new community on the village of Baldwinsville.

The board's "suggested principles to guide sound development" were described in nine points. The ultraconservative position of each "taking care of his own" was put forth by demanding that a community should assume responsibility for constructive response to inevitable growth. Other contentious points of HOCA's plan dealt with a community having free choice of economic conditions for local residents and the avoidance of harmful competition between communities. UDC was urged to abandon subsidized low-income housing in favor of more efficient methods of producing housing. ("Don't work hard

28. *Ibid*, p. 2.

at providing free housing for THEM, but promote lower cost housing through building innovations.") The fact that UDC was created simultaneously with a UDC Research Corporation actively involved in this type of effort escaped the HOCA researchers. One of HOCA's points was that ongoing maintenance of housing was as important as initial provision of facilities. Mildly insinuating that UDC was building housing projects and then abandoning them as future slums, the report supported individual homeowners and appealed to basic economic fears of local residents. In concluding their suggested principles, the board identified the need for community involvement in the development process to adapt the preliminary work of UDC in order to gain public acceptance of the plan. Addressing itself to local problems that required assistance, the plan ignored any specific proposals or methods of implementation, preferring to subjugate UDC to a coordinating group of fifty local groups ranging from town government to the Loyal Order of Moose. This approach to planning would place UDC in the role of servant; that is, UDC would pay for local ideas and implement community proposals.

In the opinion of several influential people in the Baldwinsville area and Syracuse, publication of the plan probably was the turning point of public support away from HOCA. The transparency, contradictions, and base appeals made by HOCA created an air of discredit for its earlier objectives. No longer could one be of open mind on support of HOCA. It was clear that the group could not contend with the lucid and cogent arguments of UDC. The early publicity lead held by the Homeowners' Association was lost, and UDC now had the advantage of time to persuade public opinion prior to a public hearing. Davis of UDC found the way clear to convince uninformed local residents of UDC's sincerity. The only avenue for local opposition was to contest the constitutionality of UDC in the courts.

Chester Smith had approached individual members of the local village and town boards about their interest in opposing UDC in the courts soon after the first rumors of the project began in 1969. After discussions with local political leaders, town and village representatives recognized: (1) that there was little opportunity for success against UDC in the courts, and (2) that much more political capital could be made by gaining favorable concessions from UDC in a negotiating situation. The absence of any political support led the Homeowners' Association to make a public appeal for support of a test of UDC's constitutionality in the courts. This appeal was to parallel the constructive criticism of the UDC planning work.

Smith's timetable for a suit against UDC was set to reach a peak of interest before the formal UDC public hearing on the project. Although not coincidental, UDC postponed the hearing from the fall of 1970 indefinitely into the future. It was finally held on May 17, 1971. Logue and the Metropolitan Development Association staff were prepared to gamble that they could mount a program of public relations sufficient to overcome any local opposition.

The concept of a legal test of the Urban Development Corporation surfaced in the early publicity of the Homeowners' Association in late 1969. However, HOCA's discussions with local government for support of this strategy proved fruitless. Smith recognized that without local government support he could not exert partisan political pressure on UDC. In private he admitted that "a statewide organized, a grass-roots movement, is the only way UDC can be stopped now."[29] Although the lack of any real hope of success for such a contest was becoming apparent to HOCA's board of directors, they nevertheless initiated a public appeal for support. A mail and telephone survey was conducted to determine responses to the following suggestions:

A. I prefer to have HOCA hire a lawyer to contest the legality of UDC and its Lysander project in court. I would contribute $_____ to legal expenses.
B. I prefer to have HOCA attempt to get UDC to make changes in its tentative NEW COMMUNITY PLAN for Lysander that would meet the approval of the Lysander Planning Board.
C. I would like to see HOCA contest the legality of UDC and its Lysander project if UDC will not change its Plan.[30]

The survey took several months to complete and required three efforts at canvassing. Responses were claimed from over 500 families out of a total membership of 600 families. HOCA stated that over 30 percent preferred legal action, and almost $10,000 was pledged for support. Smith concluded that members were gener-

29. The grass-roots movement alludes to a "taxpayer-revolt," a phrase used repeatedly in Syracuse newspaper editorials and in Letters to the Editor.
30. *Baldwinsville Messenger*, April 23, 1970.

ally well informed about UDC and the new-community project and wanted to contest the legality of UDC in court. Encouraged by this analysis, Smith and the board of directors decided that even though $10,000 in pledges was $15,000 short of the projected $25,000 necessary to support a lawsuit, other sources should be explored. On August 20, Smith announced a fund-raising organization for a proposed court action to test the legality of UDC for all taxpayers in New York State: "We invite assistance from individuals and community groups in other parts of New York State."[31] All of the publicity material carried Smith's name and address for directing of inquiries. Almost six months later, the Homeowners' Association announced retention of an attorney, John B. Carroll of Cazenovia, New York, and a total of "nearly" $5,000 in pledges. However, a retainer of $2,000 had to be provided from loans made by HOCA members.[32]

The Homeowners' Association called public attention to the legal approach to limiting UDC's plans in Lysander by broadening the base of political interest to a statewide level: Smith and other HOCA directors spoke before other legislative groups across the state, although they seldom appeared as speakers in their home county and towns.

HOCA's effectiveness was dampened by two actions in May, 1970. The first of these came as the result of a HOCA request for the Lysander town board to prohibit the UDC public hearing on May 17. Along with the request for postponement, the board was asked to initiate several actions limiting UDC's powers. This approach became an outright political controversy between Smith and the town board. The board rejected the request. Smith was accused of trying to get the town to shoulder expenses and carry forward a cause that was unjustified. Supervisor Van Wie said that he viewed the move as an attempt on the part of HOCA "to get us to carry the ball for them."[33] He added that he had heard that HOCA had not been able to finance a legal action against UDC.

The second action was the denial of the State Supreme Court to

31. *Ibid.*, Aug. 20, 1970.
32. *Ibid.*, Jan. 7, 1971. At one meeting Attorney Carroll admitted to a pessimistic attitude: "If we were to judge the outcome by the resources against us, we should surrender immediately. It will be a bruising fight."
33. *Ibid.*, May 6, 1971.

serve any injunction on UDC which would delay the public hearing. The hearing was held on May 17, 1971, and, on June 29, the UDC board of directors approved the project for development. HOCA's plea to the Lysander town planning board to recommend that the UDC board reject the plan was ignored. At this point virtually all organized resistance to the Lysander New Community came to an end. The last effort at resistance, the lawsuit opposing UDC, was denied by the Appellate Division of the State Supreme Court on December 8, 1971. The court found that HOCA's petition failed to establish reason for the granting of consent for a suit.

UDC's Strategy of Persuasion

While Chester Smith and the Homeowners' board of directors were vainly trying to stir up opposition, UDC's public relations efforts concentrated on resolving possible local concerns prior to the public hearing. UDC had hired the Syracuse University Research Corporation (SURC) to prepare several studies showing the probable impact of Lysander New Community on the Greater Baldwinsville area.[34] Reports of SURC identified three points of local concern for subsequent UDC action: (1) the need for reimbursement to communities for tax revenues lost through state acquisition of land; (2) the burden on schools; and (3) the future of the village of Baldwinsville. These were "gut" economic issues and represented the highest stakes for local residents.

SURC observed that in the absence of organized sentiment favoring the new community, the opposition of the Greater Baldwinsville Homeowners' and Civic Association could seriously threaten the early completion and cost of development, if not the ultimate outcome, of the project. SURC stated:

that it can be expected that the Association will move toward sorting out the issues, selecting one or two around which public opinion can coalesce, and building its confrontations on these. However Lysander residents will look to community leaders—their elected officials—for guidance, and the great strength of the Urban Development Corporation's case will be developed with the backing of this leadership. The opening of an office in Baldwinsville by the Urban Development Corporation is,

34. SURC, *The Lysander New Community.* This two-volume report, published June 15, 1969, guided UDC in many judgments on local attitudes and policy decisions to compromises with local community leaders.

of course, an important step in informing residents about the program yet one must ask if long-term credibility can be established without the support of area leaders.[35]

One of the Homeowners' Association's strongest issues was that 2,700 acres would be removed from the tax rolls by the new community. This argument could not be ignored by UDC and MDA because of its prominence and factuality. Chester Smith of HOCA relied upon this factor in his public and private discussions on the project. Considerable negotiating between local and state UDC management and local Republican political leaders drew State Senator Tarky Lombardi and State Assemblyman John Terry into the discussion. A legislative bill was drafted which would require UDC to reimburse local governments for tax revenues lost as a result of state acquisition of land. An extraordinary measure in the general framework of governmental land acquisition, the bill, nevertheless, was approved by the legislature and signed by the governor on May 20, 1970. The terms of the bill required UDC to reimburse the town of Lysander and the Baldwinsville School District in a sum equal to 100 percent of average annual property tax for the three prior years. Appropriate publicity attended the presentation of checks for approximately $25,000 to the county, town, and schools. Local media were on hand as State Senator Lombardi presented checks for 1969 and 1970 to each representative on March 4, 1971. UDC's direct cash payment was powerful public relations.

Supporting UDC's recognition of this sensitive issue was an overall long-run tax-impact study prepared by Robert Gladstone and Associates.[36] Gladstone's study was reported in the local press headlines as predicting that the new community would be a "tax boon" in that it would create profits for the local taxing units. The new tax revenue would come from taxation of private development, as land was sold to developers and was improved in accordance with the project plan. The report's conclusion was widely circulated and quoted in later presentations by UDC: "The Lysander New Community's tax revenues, at the present

35. Ibid., pp. II–7, 8.
36. Robert Gladstone and Associates, Lysander New Community Tax Impact Study, 1971.

tax rates will yield a significant tax benefit to the local citizens—with revenues exceeding costs by substantial margins as LNC development progresses." It was considered one of the most effective elements in the UDC public relations campaign.

As other issues surfaced, and opposition seemed to be jelling into a controversy, UDC acted quickly and positively. The response to HOCA charges of "killing" downtown Baldwinsville was countered by a SURC impact study financed by UDC and directed at determining how the new community would affect the village. Study findings concluded that with redevelopment the village could create a commerical and retail center which would complement rather than compete with Lysander. The public relations benefits of this approach are notable. Over eighty village business owners were contacted and interviewed by a staff member of SURC. This group represented an influential sector of the community, and their general opinion of the program was favorable. Logue promised support for a central business district study, including technical and financial aid. UDC later offered to assist the village in updating its master plan and in preparing development programs.

Similarly, schools, fire protection, and utilities were debated. In each case UDC set up task forces to meet with local representative bodies. This approach demonstrated a successful technique for coping with opposition. UDC identified an issue and publicly examined the subject. In some cases, such as schools, the local body received substantial consulting advice without cost. Study findings were widely disseminated and discussed, creating a favorable public image as conclusions were acted upon by definite policy measures, including financing by UDC. In many ways, the process of dealing with the local library or the Belgium-Cold Springs Fire District in this fashion enabled UDC to gain acceptance and credibility with local interest groups. William Marcus of UDC and John Searles of MDA agreed upon a strategy of facing an issue, developing public involvement in a study of the subject, and offering UDC assistance in implementing study conclusions. This technique reintroduced Logue as a cooperative executive who would respond to reason and dispense state largesse to the community. Time now was used in UDC's favor as community support increased, and the Homeowners' Association's arguments were eliminated prior to the public hearing.

Two factors which were part of the total environment and could influence acceptance or rejection of the project were media attitudes and scandal. Success or failure of an urban development proposal can be dependent upon the support of local press and other communications media. In a related fashion disclosure of financial scandal or political collusion involving participants in a project can spell disaster. Newspapers and television-radio media in upstate New York are conservative; over some issues they have struck a moderate point of view: they zealously guard the taxpayer from wasteful excesses of government.

With this in mind, UDC treated the local media cautiously. Syracuse newspapers were the responsibility of the Metropolitan Development Association, and the *Baldwinsville Messenger* the general responsibility of Irwin Davis. The *Messenger* meant the editor, Charles A. Baker. Conservative in attitude, Baker was honest and fair in his treatment of UDC and the new community. One must recognize the character and influence of the small-town weekly: it is a newspaper, a community notice board, a confirmer of rumor, and has the potential to greatly influence local opinion. Baker, fortunately for UDC, was as good a small-town editor as UDC could hope for. Close following of Baker's editorials from the first announcement of the new community in 1969 to the start of construction in 1973 shows he reflected local concern over taxes, home rule, and lack of information. As UDC provided convincing evidence of sincerity and earnestness, Chester Smith continued to lose credibility by his public activities. The *Messenger* editorially supported the new community, with reservations, prior to the public hearing in May, 1971. The lack of mention of Baldwinsville in public relations material irked Baker, and he said so editorially. UDC's opinion of Baker is shown by the quick response Logue offered by apologizing for the oversight and promising to rectify the matter.[37] All in all, it can be said that the local media treated UDC and the new-community project objectively and fairly. Strong ties of the Metropolitan Development Association with local media were favorable to the project, and Baker upheld the best traditions of small-town weekly newspapers.

On the issue of scandal, as hard as HOCA tried to find adverse

37. *Baldwinsville Messenger*, Aug. 25, 1971.

evidence, the project was clear of any questionable ethics or practices. When Chester Smith unearthed a windfall profit in a related UDC land purchase he presented this information to Baker. Baker confirmed the material with the town assessor and then published a strong editorial questioning UDC's fiscal management and its attitude toward public spending. Baker was plainly miffed by UDC's not directly responding to his inquiries about the subject, so he pressed the issue in print. UDC officials recognized their oversight, apologized to Baker, and honestly admitted they had been taken advantage of. Baker accepted this answer, and the issue never reappeared. Through five years of project planning, land acquisition, and site development, the project was clear of scandal. This is a remarkable public record.

Summary

A public hearing is required for proposals for urban development that involve changes in land-use controls, expenditures of public funds in land development, or introduction of new public services. Such a forum provides legislators with an insight into local attitudes toward a proposal. The Urban Development Corporation enabling legislation mandates a public hearing, although the findings of a hearing or, in fact, those of a local government, may be overruled by UDC's board of directors. Effectiveness of the public hearing notwithstanding, it permits the clearest expression of local sentiment toward a proposal.

Both the record of the hearing[38] and the *Report to the Directors of UDC*[39] summarize the events of the hearing. The hearing for Lysander, held on May 17, 1971, was attended by over 400 persons, and lasted four and one-half hours. By UDC reckoning the hearing was a success. Opposition came from the Homeowners' Association, in the person of Smith, Attorney Carroll, and other members. Smith failed to stir the crowd, and his presentation of HOCA's opposition was overshadowed by the expressions of support for the new community. UDC and MDA were well pre-

38. UDC, *Public Hearing*, held at Baker High School, Baldwinsville, New York, May 17, 1971, before Hon. John Farnham, Hearing Officer, pursuant to Section 16(2) of the New York State UDC Act on the General Project Plan for the Lysander New Community Multi-Purpose Project.

39. UDC, *Report to the Directors, Lysander New Community Public Hearing*, June 15, 1971.

pared with an array of respected and articulate representatives from county government, planning boards, chambers of commerce, and the Community Advisory Committee, as well as the mayor of Baldwinsville. Support from local government and the CAC was definite, but conditional on UDC's assurances of a favorable impact on the village and surrounding area. It was clear from discussions with observers and participants in the meeting that UDC had been successful in overcoming local opposition and had avoided community conflict over the proposal.

To assist in comparability of events in each of the case studies, we shall summarize events in relation to three central issues: (1) leadership of the developer; (2) nature or source of the proposal; and (3) method of proposal presentation to the public.

Leadership of the Developer. The Urban Development Corporation is identified by its relationship to New York State in the first order and only secondarily with characteristics of its own executive. Logue's reputation as a city builder (and to some extent a city destroyer from some of his Boston renewal projects) preceded him into New York. In the opinion of local participants in the new-community development process Logue never emerged as a symbol or public image of the agency. Logue was held in awe during his local visits primarily because of the power he represented rather than for the views he expressed in public appearances. His infrequent presence in the community made it apparent that his participation was ceremonial. Although UDC public relations provided high exposure for Logue as its chief executive, he had structured an organization for implementing programs on a statewide basis that was dependent upon managerial skills and not charismatic leadership. Besides, Governor Rockefeller generally assumed this role, as he did effectively in the passage of the agency's enabling legislation.

Logue's effectiveness as a leader in the area of urban development was a contributing factor in the community acceptance of the project. This cannot be construed as evidence of his abilities as a charismatic leader, but awareness of his influence gained adherents among the "agents of progress" in county political and business circles. There is general agreement among influential local participants in the project that Logue's identity with the state's power was of greater significance than his strengths at interpersonal relations or his personality. His prestige and affiliation established him as the final authority on compromises and concessions.

An aspect of project leadership is whether the proposal is "personalized" by identification with a leader or whether it retains a corporate identity. The transition from corporate identity to identification with individuals emerged as local representatives of the UDC began to function in the community. Irwin Davis, though not the "leader" for the UDC, established a personal identity for the agency and was able to overcome the antagonism created in the community by the group of UDC representatives that preceded him. It was reported by many people interviewed that Davis' presence created a satisfactory image for the project. So, it appears that an organization can be "personalized" by representatives who may have a greater effect than a titular leader, remote from the day-to-day activity. Rhetoric and publicity handouts do not provide the lasting impression of a casual conversation held at the pace and interest of the listener.

Nature or Source of Proposal. A study of the proposal phase at Lysander allowed us the opportunity to see whether characteristics of the organization influenced emergence of controversy, with particular reference to proposals put forth by public agencies. Observations indicate that in Lysander, where the innovator was the state, the Urban Development Corporation was looked upon with such inevitability that the project was never contested by local government, or business or political leaders. In fact, the proposal was viewed as having a high probability of success because it was backed by the financial resources of New York State. It appears that the public's perception of the innovator's ability to undertake and complete the proposal weighted acceptance toward the developer, the UDC. This case bears out the thesis that the personalization of a developer, as performed here by Davis, is essential to minimizing controversy. The campaign for public information mounted by the innovator must balance emphasis on the resources and continuity of the organization with personalization of its leaders. The approach that introduces individuals will have to gamble on public acceptance of project leaders.

Predictability of acceptance of the Lysander project was possible within only a few months after announcement of the UDC Staff Progress Report. Acceptance was due more to the ineptness of the leadership of the opposition than to the plan originating with a state agency. The arguments against low-income housing and loss of home rule were presented poorly by the Home-owners' Association so that the factor of impersonality of state government was not evident.

Method of Proposal Presentation to Public. Style versus substance in the context of public acceptance, be it a product, urban development, or a president[40] is a regular factor in American life. The methods of presenting a land-development proposal to a community must consider the characteristics of the audience, the timing and sequence of events, the appearance of and distribution of material, and the selection of effective participants for the presentation. An extended period for community review and opportunities for public scrutiny tend to militate against proposals that are dependent more on style than substance. (However, in a well-financed campaign, it is possible to conceal a land-development proposal based on incomplete detail or substantive inaccuracy.)[41]

New York State projected for Lysander New Community a well-conceived plan for public presentation in terms of appearance, content, and timing. It will be recalled that the entire project almost stumbled at the outset because of the exclusion of local residents from the decision-making process. If a vote had been required by a local government for any aspect of the project in its early months, local leaders are doubtful of its success.[42] UDC had decided that early release of information or premature discussions with area representatives would cause the project to collapse due to rampant land speculation. Other new-community developers have faced the same issue and decided to risk full commitment to a project in secrecy and gamble that the community's lack of information would not be a source of opposition. The UDC took this risk and succeeded. Eventual incorporation of community groups into the process proved to be a factor in support of local acceptance. Resolving differences in public discussions did have a direct influence on the favorable outcome of the proposal.

40. Joe McGinnis, *The Selling of the President, 1968* (New York: Trident, 1969).
41. SURC made this observation in its first report, *The Lysander New Community,* Vol. I.
42. *New York Times,* News of the Week, July 1, 1973.

The Urban Development Corporation showed its strongest points in overcoming local opposition when faced with the economic issues of taxes, schools, and the future of the village of Baldwinsville. UDC was able to resolve each controversial point by crystallizing an issue and then bringing it to the point of negotiation. Through its ability to directly influence special enabling legislation through the governor's office, UDC could reach a level of satisfaction for local claims. However, it is undoubtedly the state's ability to provide direct cash subsidies for payments in lieu of taxes, school aid grants, or support for urban renewal planning that enabled the public corporation to reduce local opposition. These measures are not within the province of private developers who are constrained by an inability to influence special legislation or disrupt tenuous cash-flow situations for disbursements not directly related to physical development. Problems of this nature plague private developers, as we shall see in the case studies of the next two chapters.

4 | Gananda

During late 1968 and early 1969, when Logue was committing the New York State Urban Development Corporation (UDC) to the new community of Lysander, Stewart Moot began to formulate plans for a new town near Rochester. Moot felt that farmland in neighboring Wayne County could be assembled for development at lower costs than in Rochester's rapidly urbanizing Monroe County. With little previous experience in land development, Moot set aside his law practice and committed himself to acquiring almost 10,000 acres of land, developing plans, and starting a project which could create an "ideal community" for 80,000 people when completed thirty years later.

Moot's proposal for Gananda was well received locally with little controversy or public criticism shown, as in the case of Lysander. In contrast to Lysander, however, Gananda did not have the financing or administrative support provided there by UDC. This lack of support created a gradually developing form of resistance, not from individuals or community groups, but from elected officials and employees of public agencies. The story of Gananda's successful strategy of persuasion to avoid conflict and its subsequent reversals are described in this chapter.

Project Description

Gananda is the Seneca Indian word for "new settlement." The developer had this in mind when he set out to purchase the land necessary for the project. The site is approximately twelve miles east of downtown Rochester, in the towns of Walworth and Macedon in southwestern Wayne County (see Figure 4.1). The site includes approximately 10,500 acres. Of this land, Moot proposed to develop 8,705 acres; the remainder was intended for public use, and there were a few scattered parcels which the developer did not control. For comparison, Lysander is 2,700 acres, Reston 6,750 acres, and Columbia is 15,000 acres.

In contrast to the single purchase of land at Lysander, Moot had to secure land in the pattern used by James Rouse for Columbia. Separate negotiations were held with 110 owners. Options were taken in 1970 and 1971, and purchases were completed in 1972. Per-acre prices varied, depending on location and quality of the site, but average costs were about $1,000 per acre. All but a few of the purchases were made from active farmers, many of whom were descendants of the original settlers.[1] The lack of controversy at the first announcement of the project is attributable to the characteristics of the people of the area. Site residents and property owners were unsophisticated in matters of speculative land development. Few had selected the area as a place of exurban refuge, and the people of the area tended to be independent individualists, adhering primarily to existing social institutions.

Wayne County, New York, celebrated its 150th anniversary in 1973. For many years the population of this agriculturally oriented county fluctuated around 50,000 persons. After the early 1950's population growth introduced some of the problems of urbanization. Situated between Syracuse and Rochester on Lake Ontario, the area has remained oriented to its rich fruit orchards and muckland. The western part of the county became a site for Rochester exurbanites in the late 1950's and early 1960's. The development and rapid expansion of the Xerox Corporation in the 1960's, in adjacent Monroe County contiguous to the western towns of Wayne County, generated small subdivisions. The three western towns, Ontario, Macedon, and Walworth had a total

---

1. At the time of site purchases there were 468 residents on site, 63 of them over 60 years old; there were 54 working farms, and 16 that were occupied but were not being worked. Located on the site were 127 nonfarm residences. See HUD, Office of New Communities Development, *Environmental Impact Statement on the Proposed Gananda New Community, Wayne County, New York* (Washington, D.C., Feb. 8, 1972), p. 13.

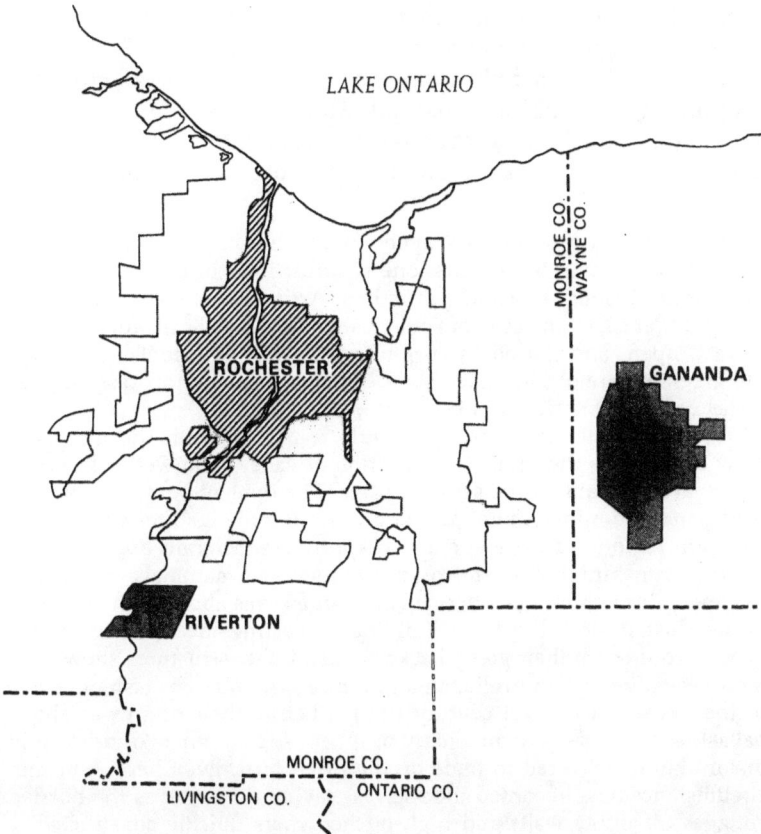

Figure 4.1. Map of Gananda and environs

population of 16,086 in the 1970 census. The town of Ontario grew by approximately 2,000 in the period from 1970 to 1973. The town of Walworth had only 2,782 persons in 1960. By 1970 its population had grown to 4,584, a 64.8 percent increase. Much of this growth occurred after a water line was installed in the town in 1965. Macedon grew by 50 percent between the two censuses, while the village of Macedon went from 645 people in 1960 to 1,168 in 1970 for an 81.1 percent growth.

Farmers who sold land to the subdividers were envied by their neighbors as having found a successful means of acquiring a retirement stake, a position many other property owners in the same age range were hoping to find.

The land itself is hilly farmland and wooded area. Hills are drumlin formations, and natural watercourses and some wetlands exist. Small farms, scattered private homes, and rural hamlets comprise the site's present use. But note the developer's rhetoric:

Crossing from Monroe to Wayne County, through the major visual gateway of flanking woodlands, one is thrust into the multiple undulations of north-south traversing drumlins. Arrival is complete! The fact is brought home like an ocean of land crashing upon walls of woodlands. It is vast, open, and graced by magnificent stands of woodlands against the green texture of unbroken vistas. From strategic points one may see vistas of Lake Ontario and Rochester in the distance.

Descending the drumlins is a gentle transition from the unbroken view of miles, to the intimate perception of valleys and wetlands, creating a naturally captivating sense of place. The opulent landscape of wetland ponds, in mid-summer almost duplicating the lush foliage of more southern regions, is close enough to appreciate. Migrant ducks dot the ponds in unassuming accent to smaller fowl and mammals common to the area. Throughout the site small and large farms abound; their picturesque clusters of old red out-buildings reflecting the intensity of the sun, in contrast to their green backgrounds. Other structures show their more recent vintage in brilliant aluminum. In less obvious fashion, some of the houses of the last century's farms betray their origins as ship's ballast, some made of sedimentary or igneous rock, others of brick from distant kilns, delivered in trade on the Erie Canal. Even here, time and circumstance have recorded themselves, saving for our eyes the hurried cottages of rubble walls and high-pitched roofs quickly constructed to shelter against the advent of piercing cold and enveloping snow. The craftsman skills of Colonial architecture have provided the delicate proportions of a scattering of homes. These elements come together in the village of Macedon Center in the south-central site. It is a brief interlude of historic charm with accenting church steeples marking a village existence, given formal expression in the light sprinkling of Greek Revival buildings. To the extreme south of the site are rail lines, linked through the site in the nineteenth century along the route of the Erie Barge Canal, which creates the southern site boundary.[2]

The developer's goals and policies did not receive the same thorough scrutiny as the plans for Lysander, probably because of

2. Quoted in the New Wayne Communities, Inc., Title VII submission, *Program Plan, Volume B* (Oct., 1971), p. 170.

the private sponsorship of the project.[3] If public monies had been involved, the detailed statements on social goals for the project might have been subject to criticism. This would have been disappointing to the developer who placed emphasis in the planning documents on the social objectives of the proposal. Original planning goals were stated as:

1. To create a new community in which it is possible for people to be representative of a cross-section of economic groups in the total Rochester community, with an emphasis on the moderate and middle-income ranges.
2. To create a new community which serves the interests and needs of such an economic cross-section of residents.
3. To create a new community whose amenities and services for all families are extensive and of high quality.
4. To create a new community of sufficient size to have significant social and economic impact on the entire region within which it is developed.
5. To create a new community which overturns the social assumptions inherent in virtually all traditional real estate development, and which provides a model alternative to urban decay and suburban sprawl.[4]

Firm belief in these goals is reinforced by the statement on social consequences of the project included in the Environmental Impact Statement prepared by HUD:

Of all the new community applications received to date by the Office of New Communities Development, GANANDA's is the only one in which all social planning was completed prior to the initiation of land use planning. Further, the social plan was taken into consideration during all phases of the community layout planning process. The Office of the New Communities Development believes this to be a most appropriate procedure for new community planning, and sees it as characteristic of the Developer's serious intent to plan for people.[5]

3. Letter to the author from Mr. Robinson Lapp, a project manager for Gananda.
4. *Program Plan, Volume A*, p. 50.
5. HUD, Office of New Communities Development, *Environmental Impact Statement*, p. 21. The application process for the developer to obtain federal guarantees under Title VII of the Housing and Urban Development Act of 1970 requires compliance "with the provisions of Public Law 91-190 (The Natural Environmental Policy Act of 1969) regarding public and agency review of the impact of new community projects upon environmental quality." Compliance is represented by the preparation of an Environmental Impact Statement by HUD.

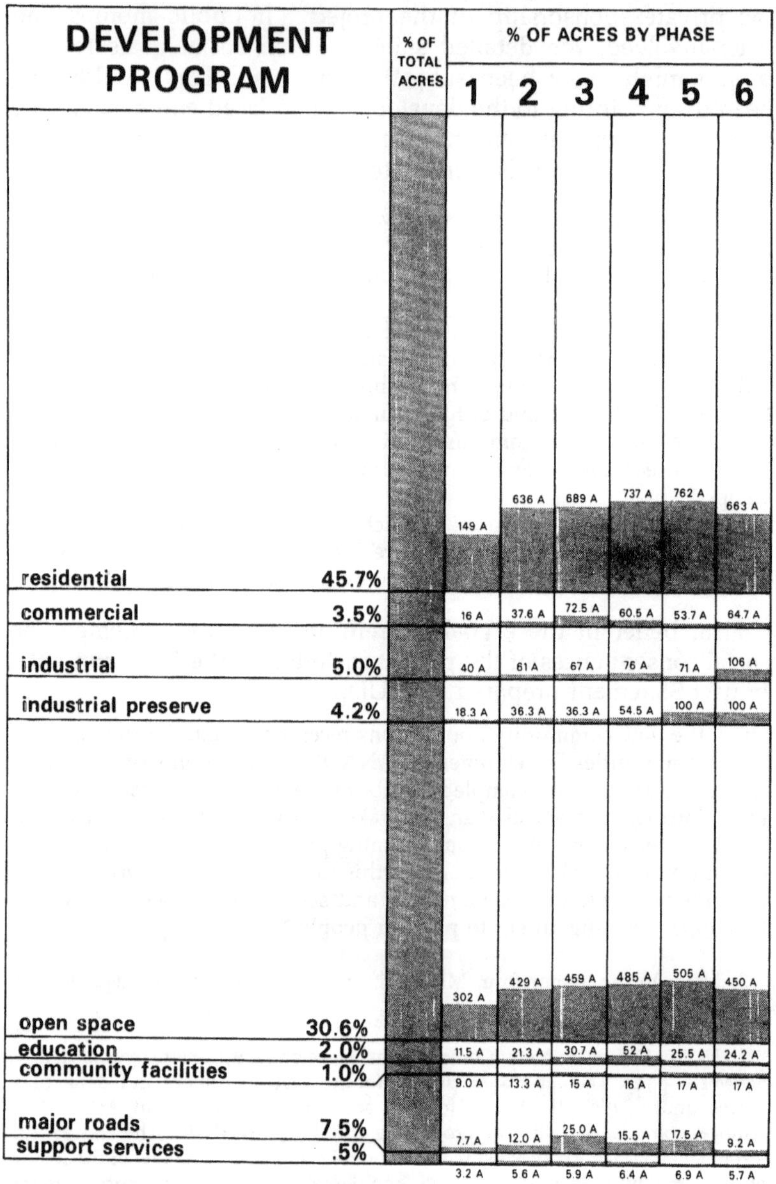

DEVELOPMENT PROGRAM	% OF TOTAL ACRES	% OF ACRES BY PHASE					
		1	2	3	4	5	6
residential	45.7%	149 A	636 A	689 A	737 A	762 A	663 A
commercial	3.5%	16 A	37.6 A	72.5 A	60.5 A	53.7 A	64.7 A
industrial	5.0%	40 A	61 A	67 A	76 A	71 A	106 A
industrial preserve	4.2%	18.3 A	36.3 A	36.3 A	54.5 A	100 A	100 A
open space	30.6%	302 A	429 A	459 A	485 A	505 A	450 A
education	2.0%	11.5 A	21.3 A	30.7 A	52 A	25.5 A	24.2 A
community facilities	1.0%	9.0 A	13.3 A	15 A	16 A	17 A	17 A
major roads	7.5%	7.7 A	12.0 A	25.0 A	15.5 A	17.5 A	9.2 A
support services	.5%	3.2 A	5.6 A	5.9 A	6.4 A	6.9 A	5.7 A

Figure 4.2. Gananda development program: Land-use distribution

Table 4.1. Gananda thirty-year development plan

	1973–1977 Phase I	1978–1982 Phase II	1983–1987 Phase III	1988–1992 Phase IV	1993–1997 Phase V	1998–2002 Phase VI	Total
Acreage development	914	1,332	1,569	1,609	1,665	1,512	8,600
Population	8,461	12,357	14,652	16,560	17,170	16,600	85,000
Dwelling units	2,385	3,680	4,535	5,300	5,500	5,500	26,900
On-site employment*	1,130	2,230	2,930	2,710	2,500	3,000	14,500
Family centers	3	3	3	4	3	4	20
Community centers	1	1		1	1		4
Regional center		Commercial			Community facilities		

Source: Gananda Program Plan, Volume B, p. 229.
*Does not include construction employment.

The development program is organized into six five-year phases, illustrated in Figure 4.2 and Table 4.1. At completion there will be 26,900 dwelling units, and 14,500 on-site employment opportunities will be available. Residential mix is described as including 34 percent of total housing stock for sale or rental in the low- and moderate-income housing range. The developer's data do not explicitly state "public" housing but describe the "household distribution" in income terms. Of the 34 percent low- and moderate-income housing (as defined by HUD) it can be computed that 16 percent of the total will be in "assisted" housing. The developer's approach to explaining this low amount (compared to 30 percent at Lysander) is to state that

Table 4.2. Comparison of income per household in Gananda and in Rochester metropolitan area

Income per household unit	Percent of population in Gananda	Percent of population in Rochester metropolitan area
Up to $10,000	39%	40.3%
$10,000–$15,000	36%	25.1%
$15,000 and over	25%	35.6%

Source: Environmental Impact Statement, p. 6.

"housing will be made available to be representative of the average metropolitan Rochester income range." Omitting mention of "public" housing, income distribution is described as shown in Table 4.2.

Course of Events

The idea for Gananda grew from Stewart Moot's experiences in housing development. He had previously helped the Rochester Area Council of Churches develop 450 units of nonprofit housing. His deepening involvement in improving social conditions resulted in his running for the Rochester City School Board. Although he lost, his involvement with the Presbyterian Church as clerk of the Genesee Valley Presbytery maintained his interests in social conditions at the local and regional level. This religious commitment influenced actions taken later for Gananda.

In his contacts with the church, Moot recognized that many of the property owners in western Wayne County were retired farmers or active farmers reaching retirement age. Only a fraction of the residents were people who had moved "out" from the city; the residents were closely tied to the land and retained values associated with rural living. Farmers had heard of relatives in Monroe County and in adjacent towns making "a killing" by selling their land to speculative developers. Moot convinced the property owners, who were wary of being bilked by developers, to accept purchase options for twelve months with no down payment. Moot's ability to engender confidence was basic to the success he achieved in gaining public acceptance in the beginning of the project.

Expansion of the Xerox Corporation only ten miles north of the site had created the first pressures of development in the towns of Walworth and Macedon. The town of Walworth supervisor, Charles Hack, a farmer in office since 1960, had very early convinced the town that it should be prepared to attract development by building a water line. The potential for development—a rural town with comparatively low land prices, willing sellers, and available water—was what had brought Moot to the area. Moot selected 3,000 acres and, by the fall of 1969 had engaged the services of an architectural-engineering firm. He also secured the financial support of three partners—with whom he later became disenchanted. He very early severed relations with the three men and sought other financial backers.

The curiosity of area residents became intense by September, 1969, when farmers heard rumors of land assembly and realized that many of their neighbors had signed options with Moot. Rumors were confirmed with public announcement of the proposal for development of the site—a planned community for 30,000 persons.[6] Two of Moot's earliest choices for management leadership joined him at this time. Robinson Lapp and Paul Barru were given responsibility to oversee corporate activities for New Wayne Communities, Inc., Gananda's parent organization. Lapp and Barru were experienced in the development of nonprofit housing led by church groups. Both had gravitated to this field as ordained ministers aiding local action groups, although they lacked formal training in business or real estate. Their characters were open, sincere, and expressed a basic sense of honesty that area residents could identify with and trust. As simple as this may sound, the early acceptance of the project by local communities has been attributed to the personalities of Lapp and Barru.

Although inexperienced in real estate development, Moot's management team set a timetable which coordinated property acquisition, planning, public relations, and fiscal matters. The approach Moot pursued was the involvement of professional consultants, whose participation could be supported by an equity position in the corporation in lieu of cash payment. Moot had read the publicity concerning British new towns and their planners, and his knowledge led him to discuss possible arrangements with two firms, Lansdown Holt and Partners, and Hugh Wilson and Lewis Wormsley. Both firms also represented financial investors potentially interested in backing Gananda. Holding onto his land options, and acquiring more, Moot negotiated with the overseas firms through the end of 1969 and into early 1970. For undisclosed reasons, these negotiations proved unsuccessful and in the spring of 1970 New Wayne Communities reevaluated its strategy. It was decided to seek financial and professional support locally, in Syracuse and Rochester.

Two of the country's larger architectural-planning and engi-

6. *Rochester Times-Union*, Sept. 10, 1969.

neering firms are located in Syracuse. Both run big construction programs and have contacts in the region for financial backers. After considering the project, the architectural firm decided not to become involved, but the engineering firm accepted the offer. Both agreed that the project's inexperienced management increased the risk, but different objectives for professional services resulted in different conculsions. For further professional assistance Moot expanded outside the local area. Retained for the preparation of a plan for local review and submission to HUD was Richard P. Browne Associates of Columbia, Maryland. This firm had evolved from the group that designed Columbia and was concurrently involved in other new-town projects. Moot also introduced Russell Deeter of Pittsburgh to the project. Deeter, president of the architectural-planning firm of Deeter, Ritcher, Sippel Associates, saw prospects for professional commissions as well as possibilities for speculative investment. By the summer of 1970 New Wayne Communities had secured strong financial backing of over a million dollars from local Rochester sources. This is reflected in the composition of the board of directors: all but two of the thirteen members are from Wayne and Monroe counties.[7] A planning timetable was established with a submission to HUD scheduled for fall of 1971, with construction to start by spring of 1973.

Planning continued through 1970 and into early 1971. Moot had been able to extend all of his purchase options under original conditions for another year. By this time he had options for 91 percent of the 8,705 acres contained in the project area. The remainder of the land was under active acquisition. Press reactions were favorable all during this period, and no evidence of local controversy appeared.[8]

Two extraordinary events occurred in April, 1971. On the first of April, a joint resolution of the supervisors, town boards, and town planning boards of Macedon and Walworth was adopted,

7. This action affected the project in several significant ways. First, it gave the project a measure of credibility to area residents and governmental representatives because of the prominence of the supporters. Second, it eventually caused a restructuring of management of New Wayne Communities as a result of the close scrutiny possible by proximity to the project's daily operations.

8. The two Rochester newspapers, the *Democrat and Chronicle*, and the *Times-Union*, have continually supported the project, with minor exceptions, and have provided several major serialized articles on the project.

pledging unanimous support for the Gananda concept. The resolution called for public hearings and for support in expediting the development of the new community, if approved by both town governments. On the second of April the board of supervisors and planning board for Wayne County passed resolutions supporting New Wayne Communities.

Public hearings were held for zoning of Gananda lands in Macedon on June 29 and in Walworth on July 30, 1971. On July 15, the concepts and provisions for the New Community District Zoning Ordinance were worked out and agreed upon at joint meetings of the planning and town boards for Macedon and Walworth and New Wayne Communities. The joint ordinance creating a new-community district of 10,500 acres extending over parts of both townships was approved by both planning boards. The ordinance was published, public hearings were held, and approval without dissent was given by both town boards. (See Appendix for the Macedon-Walworth New Community District Zoning Ordinance.)

Moot and his backers were now confident as they prepared to obtain approval from the A-95 regional representatives: the Genesee-Finger Lakes Regional Planning Board and the New York State Planning and Development Clearinghouse, Office of Planning Coordination.[9] This process was the last step prior to filing for Title VII assistance. What had Moot accomplished at this point in time? He could legitimately claim very strong public and community support. With little experience in the development field and even less in the way of private capital, Moot had put together a program with apparent unlimited potential for suc-

9. The Intergovernmental Cooperation Act of 1968 sets forth requirements for coordination of direct federal development programs and projects with state, regional, and local planning programs. The Office of Management and Budget (OMB), Executive Office of the President, issued Circular A-95, effective April 1, 1971, to guide federal agencies in the coordination process. A provision of A-95 was the Project Notification and Review System requiring a network of state, regional, and metropolitan planning and development clearinghouses. The appropriate clearinghouses, in Gananda's case, were the Genesee-Finger Lakes Regional Planning Board and the New York State Planning and Development Clearinghouse, Office of Planning Coordination. See "Project Review and Notification System: Regional Clearinghouse Procedures" (Mimeographed; Genesee-Finger Lakes Regional Planning Board, June, 1971). See also *Circular A-95* (Washington, D.C.: Executive Office of the President, Office of Management and Budget, Feb. 9, 1971).

cess. There had been no public resistance to the project. New Wayne Communities had only to receive the regional clearing-house approval.

The review process was outlined to start on August 2, 1971, and be completed on September 16 to meet an October date for presentation to HUD. For the first time in the project's short history it ran into resistance. The regional planning board, influenced by members from nearby Monroe and Ontario counties, objected to portions of the proposed plan. The review process was rescheduled for the period October 8 to December 20. It was a serious and unexpected blow when the Monroe County Planning Council requested an extension of the review into early January. Time became critical for Moot, as his purchase options would come due within four to six months and any delay would cause him serious difficulties in land acquisition.

The shock was great, therefore, when the executive director of the Council, William Uptegrove sent HUD a letter on January 21, 1972 urging them to

delay any final consideration of this project until the developer has had an opportunity to present his proposal to the City of Rochester, the eastern towns of Monroe County and to the Monroe County Planning Council, and until the appropriate agencies representing these areas have had an opportunity to make constructive comments on the feasibility and impact of the Gananda proposal.[10]

Not only was Moot dismayed by this action, but so were the local supporters in Wayne County. Both town supervisors publicly expressed their opinions, Supervisor Hack of Walworth stating that "I think they're sticking their noses in where they shouldn't be."[11]

Local editorials bluntly accused members of the Monroe County Planning Council of being obstructionists and urged Washington (HUD) to ignore the objections and approve New Wayne Communities' application. What appeared to be a major event took shape when the Monroe County Planning Council called on Moot to address all interested parties at a meeting on

10. Letter from William T. Uptegrove, Director of Planning, County of Monroe, to Mr. Samuel C. Jackson, Asst. Secretary, U.S. Department of Housing and Urban Development, Jan. 21, 1972.
11. Quoted in the *Newark Courier-Gazette*, Feb. 2, 1972.

February 8, 1972. The result was typical of Moot's public dealings and his ability to instill a sense of trust and honesty in his presentations; the Council believed him and removed their objections. In a letter to HUD Assistant Secretary Samuel Jackson, Council Chairman Robert J. Gustafson said: "Now that we have a better understanding of the objectives of the project, we feel that the Ganada concept of a new community in Wayne County is worthy of HUD consideration." [12] On April 7, 1972, HUD announced approval of the New Wayne Communities' application for Title VII guarantee. A commitment to guarantee $22 million in loans from private sources was made under the provisions of the Housing Act of 1970.

In the early stages of planning, Moot and his management team developed a strategy for gaining local support and governmental acceptance. Indications were good for success in this aspect of project development. A report prepared in March, 1970, by the Rochester Center for Governmental and Community Research for the New York State Urban Development Corporation stated that "it [Ganada] is a very satisfactory site for essentially private development, and the political climate for the proposed development appears to be very favorable." [13]

New Wayne Communities prepared its strategy for gaining acceptance, with two areas of concentration: (1) overcoming local opposition; and (2) obtaining governmental support. Both areas were worked on simultaneously with an air of openness and a maximum amount of public disclosure. Moot repeatedly pledged: "It is the intention of the Developer to continue to engage in active conversations with all interested parties to insure as each succeeding phase of the development proceeds, local needs and concerns will continue to be addressed seriously and incorporated into the planning." [14]

Moot identified the concern of the area residents for the impact of Ganada on matters directly affecting their lives and communities as: (1) taxes; (2) the structure and relation of existing gov-

12. Letter to Secretary Jackson, from Robert T. Gustafson, Director of Planning, Feb. 14, 1972.

13. *Planned Communities for the Rochester Metropolitan Area,* March, 1970, p. 102. The report was prepared for the UDC regional office and examined eleven potential sites in the region.

14. *Program Plan, Volume A,* p. 49.

ernmental bodies to Gananda; (3) the possible overloading of existing community services including but not limited to schools; (4) the economic impact on the area; and (5) the impact of large population growth on the area.

How did New Wayne Communities address these concerns? The presence of people such as Lapp and Barru and the establishment of a site office in a restored nineteenth-century Grange Hall in Macedon Center were contributory to acceptance. By taking the town supervisors into their confidence at an early date, the developers created strong advocates for the project from the affected towns. Supervisor Hack, who later sold his farm in Walworth for $212,000, was an avid supporter from the start. His position was that development should benefit developer and community. In his own words Hack felt that "growth was inevitable, so why not have it done the way you want?" He reasoned that the town residents had recognized this by agreeing to tax themselves for a new water system in 1965:

> Hack points to a problem brought by new residents who moved from city areas and now demand the services they had there. Older rural-oriented residents, more used to doing for themselves, don't approve of spending the tax money to provide the new services. But gradually services have come. As a result, prices are skyrocketing for land. Lots which were $900 just a few years ago have whizzed up to $4,000 to $5,000 now.[15]

Town of Macedon Supervisor Augustine Marvin agreed with Hack. He has stated that "growth is inevitable but we should try to make it go in the directions most beneficial to the town."[16]

The developers repeatedly offered public assurances that all efforts would be made to plan programs for Gananda which would avoid the possibility of increased taxes for existing area residents. Recognizing that although growth would generate large increases in tax revenues, and that traditional approaches to the provision of community services would still require significant increases in local taxes, New Wayne Communities, for its part, agreed to seek specific major economies in capital expenditures and operations and to create new institutions to protect existing town residents from being taxed for Gananda improvements.

These promises were elaborated on in the report on fiscal con-

15. *Rochester Democrat and Chronicle,* Feb. 12, 1973, p. 3B.   16. *Ibid.*

siderations prepared by consultants to New Wayne Communities, Economic Research Associates.[17] The report stated that by the end of the first phase of development in 1977 a positive fiscal impact on both towns would be apparent. Macedon could expect to have an annual net benefit of $405,000, and Walworth would receive $676,000. By 1982 the amounts would increase to $901,000 in Walworth and $900,000 in Macedon, and by 1987 benefits for Walworth would be $1,750,000 and $1,646,000 for Macedon.

Tax relief for town residents from the cost of services of benefit essentially for Gananda residents was described in the consultants' report. The most important recommendation of the report was the proposal to create a new school district to be carved out of the existing two districts serving the site. For the developers to accept this recommendation involved a calculated risk, because it exposed them to a direct public referendum as required for new school proposals. The success of this unique solution to one of the most controversial issues surrounding urban land development (increased school taxes) is described in detail later in this chapter. One of the convincing actions taken by the developers was the creation of a Gananda Community Facilities Corporation to own and manage educational and community-shared facilities. This action forestalled some local questions about the likelihood that the burden of planning and operating these services would fall on existing units of government. The developers agreed, however, that taxing authority for the site would remain with presently existing municipal bodies and not be transferred to Gananda.

In order to dispel fear of "a takeover of local government" by the new community, the developers "publicly committed them-

17. Economic Research Associates' data indicated that all areas of government service would show a positive fiscal impact. This increase, the surplus of revenues after expenses are met, was computed by subtracting the cost of services provided by the town of Macedon to service Gananda residents living within Macedon from the total property tax revenues that will be generated by those residents in Gananda. Three variables determine the amount of the net fiscal impact. The first is the increase in market land values due to development operations. Second is the effect of local assessment practices and related tax rates against the assessment base which will determine the amount of tax to be collected by the town of Macedon from Gananda. The third variable is the rate at which services to the community increase. The rate is adjusted not only to the expected increase in population, but also to the increase in quality needed to provide adequate services to the community.

selves to the continuance of all existing municipal bodies to the greatest extent possible. The developer has no interest in developing any new political entities." Local response to this position was received favorably by the Wayne County board of supervisors and other elected officials.[18]

The impact of Gananda on local services, the economy, and life styles had been treated by the developers in their plans and public commitments. A consistently repeated comment about the project referred to the inevitability of population growth and the need to plan for it. United States Congressman Frank Horton remarked that "growth is inevitable and it is important that it be used to best advantage by Wayne County residents. The planned development of Gananda will insure that growth and change will come in a planned orderly fashion." [19]

One lifetime resident of Macedon Center commented: "We knew that increased housing was coming and it's better our growth be planned."

Attitudes of area residents toward the sprawling pattern of development in the Rochester metropolitan area gave support to Moot's plan in its early days. Rochester's continued growth, resulting from the strength of industries like Kodak and Xerox, assured that rural land in Wayne County would eventually be incorporated into the region. This was indicated by the expansion of the Rochester Metropolitan Statistical Area in the United States Census of 1970 to include Wayne County. Local newspapers regularly reported issues of land development, and the planning activities of governmental units were given frequent and accurate coverage.

Gananda's developers responded to critics of the project's possibly disruptive effect on the rural atmosphere of the area by describing the phased nature of the project and its proposed land-use controls. Emphasizing a thirty-year development plan (see Table 4.1), New Wayne Communities expressed concern for a gradual transition of the site from rural to urban. Through the zoning ordinance and basic land concept, the developer promised to maintain environmental quality by (1) a program of open-space development and maintenance to avoid urban congestion;

18. *Program Plan, Volume A*, p. 48.
19. See *Environmental Impact Statement*, pp. 7–25.

(2) aesthetically pleasing street and site planning to take natural features into careful consideration and create a harmonious blend with the land; and (3) prevention of strip commercial developments and sprawl of typical suburban subdivisions. These promises were adequate to remove the strongest objections to the project made in its early days, those of the Monroe County Planning Council.[20]

An issue of local concern which the developers recognized as a potential source of controversy was the removal of high-quality farmland from production. Criticism came from two groups: (1) area residents, and (2) representatives of government environmental protection agencies. Area residents who were possible sources of organized conflict over this issue were the very people who were personally benefiting from the project: the farmers. Objections to "seeing good farmland go to waste, especially with food prices going up the way they are" were overcome, because the farmers knew they could buy new farms within several miles of their old homes and clear a profit in the sale transaction.[21] Typical of these was Isaac Abraham of Walworth. He was born at his farm and started to work it in 1937. After selling his land to Gananda, he planned to buy a farm in a nearby town and continue working. Others who were retiring from farming sold off all but a house lot and planned to live out their lives on the site. This wise approach of accommodation by the developers created a force of advocates who refused to consider any attempts to protest the project.

The second source of criticism over the issue of the use of farmland was the public agencies in New York State charged with responsibility for statewide comprehensive planning. The New York State Development Plan published in 1971 described the area as containing "high viability farmland." The developers'

20. The Monroe County Planning Council's objections were that the size of the project would drastically affect land development in the eastern part of the county and have a drastic effect on the county's economy, transportation facilities, and public utilities. See Monroe County Planning Council, *Review of Draft Environmental Statement*, Jan., 1972.

21. At the public closing of options held on June 1, 1972, the farmers who were interviewed generally agreed that "there was enough good farmland to be bought in Wayne County," and the Gananda site would have been built on with "cracker boxes" anyway.

response to this point did not dispute the fact of this irreversible and irretrievable commitment of the land resource. Instead, they put forth the argument:

The issue, therefore, is not whether the conversion of this land to urban uses should occur but, rather, the manner in which it should occur. We believe that the public interest is well served through development in the form of the proposed new community as contrasted with piecemeal, sprawl development which would otherwise occur in the area. . . . Again, we believe that the public interest is well served through development in the form of the proposed new community since the use of these resources probably will be controlled more efficiently than through any other mode of development.[22]

These arguments, as well as the personal style of the developers' representatives, forestalled community controversy evolving from area residents' concerns. The strategy of persuasion adopted by New Wayne Communities in securing the approval of local government and public agencies, however, required a different approach.

Local Government and Agency Approval

The tortuous routes of government and agency approvals necessary for a new-community project were discussed in Chapter 3. At any one of the points of review and required approval, a controversial issue can be generated. Such an issue can, in turn, become the source of conflict between area residents and the developer. New Wayne Communities evaluated the hierarchy of governments and agencies they had to face. It was concluded that the key agency in the local network of town, county, and regional bodies, state agencies and federal representatives, was the A-95 regional clearinghouse, the Genesee-Finger Lakes Regional Planning Board (see Table 4.3).

Moot's success in dealing with the two town and planning boards of Walworth and Macedon had resulted in an uncontroversial public hearing and unanimous board approval in July, 1971, for an identically worded New Communities District Zoning Ordinance. This was to be administered by an eight-member Joint Preliminary Review Board. The Board's composition—two

22. See *Environmental Impact Statement*, p. 28; and Wayne County Planning Board, letter from Robert Peterson, Director, to Stewart Moot, Nov. 15, 1971.

Table 4.3. Government bodies and agencies concerned with Gananda project

Wayne County political jurisdictions
  Wayne County Planning Board
  Township of Macedon
  Township of Walworth
  School Districts:
    Palmyra-Macedon School District #1
    Wayne-Central School District #1
  Fire Districts:
    Macedon Center Fire District
    Walworth Fire Districts #1 and #2
  Water Districts:
    Macedon Water District #6
    Walworth Water District #1
Regional and area-wide social service and planning agencies (a partial list)
  Cooperative Area Manpower Planning System (CAMPS)
  Genesee-Finger Lakes Regional Planning Board
  Genesee Regional Health Planning Council
  Genesee Valley School Development Association
  New York State Department of Education, Office of Vocational Rehabilitation, Rochester District Office
  New York State Department of Health, Rochester Regional Office
  New York State Department of Mental Hygiene, Division of Local Services, Rochester Regional Office
  New York State Department of Social Service, Rochester Area Office
  New York State Division for Youth, Genesee Valley District (Rochester)
  Rochester/Genesee Regional Transportation Authority
  Rochester Regional Health and Hospital Council
  Rochester Regional Medical Program
  United States Department of Labor, MA, District Office (Rochester)

Source: Gananda Program Plan, Volume A, p. 44.

members each from the two towns, one from the Wayne County Planning Board, and three from the developers—was conceived as a buffer between local political rivalries and the developers' needs. This concept had received the blessing of the county board of supervisors and both political parties.

Support for the project at the state and the federal level was being sought simultaneously with the project review at the local level. Assistance in processing for the Title VII application was sought from United States Congressman Frank Horton. Horton was impressed with the developers' plans and agreed with what he called "certainly one of the major events in the history of Wayne County."

In July, 1971, a joint meeting was held in Congressman Horton's office, attended by Senators Jacob Javits and James Buckley, to discuss the Gananda application. Following that meeting a letter was sent to Secretary George Romney of the United States Department of Housing and Urban Development, urging that processing of the Gananda application be completed. The letter was signed by Congressman Horton and Senators Javits and Buckley.

The last major hurdles prior to submission for Title VII funding were the reviews required by the A-95 process. The Genesee-Finger Lakes Regional Planning Board and the New York State Planning and Development Clearinghouse, Office of Planning Coordination, received Gananda plans in August, 1971. By December, 1971, all appropriate agencies had responded positively, except for the Monroe County Planning Council. Feeling disturbed that Moot had not personally presented his plans to the Council, objections to the project were drawn, but Moot went before this body in February, 1972, and gained their approval.

One of the strongest elements in the developers' strategy for persuasion proved itself during this period. This element was the question of disclosure: How much information do you make public and not risk failure of the project by revealing controversial features?

New Wayne Communities developed the strategy of referring to the Gananda Project Plan as a "concept." This term is found over and over again in the developers' literature, and in newspaper articles and agency comments. As a "term of art," it allowed a broad interpretation of the specificity of the plan. At the public presentation before the joint town and planning boards in April, 1971, Moot could defend the proposal for the zoning ordinance on the grounds that it was: "based on a concept rather than on a platted street plan, thus allowing great flexibility for community planning." Moot not only resisted fixing a development plan with rigid details for thirty years off into the future, he also prevented opponents from grasping onto controversial elements for debate. What might have been called deceit or uncertainty, if not presented properly, was received as a sincere and honest statement when presented by New Wayne Communities. Confirmation of Moot's credibility is found in the Monroe County Planning Council's recommendation for approval of the project:

Gananda is still essentially a concept, much remains in choosing between alternatives and preparing detailed plans. The ultimate impact of Gananda on Monroe County will depend to a great extent on the choices that will be made between the alternatives.[23]

Through its various early stages of development the Gananda proposal generated little controversy. The developers could point out that from 1969 through Title VII approval in 1972, as the tenth new community to receive federal assistance, the project had outstanding public and community support.

In the towns of Macedon and Walworth the support from the planning board and the town boards was without precedent. The Wayne County board of supervisors, planning board, and Economic Development Corporation endorsed Gananda enthusiastically and promised support in planning, road improvement, industrial solicitations, and in creation of parks and public services. Support was also received from the local chamber of commerce, and both the Republican and Democratic parties. In its presentation to the staff of Governor Rockefeller, the chairman of the Monroe County legislature and the Monroe County Republican chairman joined with the representatives of Wayne County, including New York State Senator Thomas Laverne and Assemblyman Joseph Finley. In addition to support from Governor Rockefeller's office, Gananda also received very strong personal support from United States Congressman Frank Horton and United States Senators Jacob Javits and James Buckley.

Among the strongest influences on local opinion were the town supervisors. At the announcement of the Title VII approval, Macedon Town Supervisor Marvin stated that Gananda provides "a real opportunity for our community to carry out some of the most modern concepts of community living." Town of Walworth Supervisor Hack indicated that Gananda would be a boon to the area if it developed according to plans: "This can be really good if it is built and developed the way it is supposed to be. It can be one of the most fantastic things that ever hit this part of the country."

One last opportunity for controversy and possible community conflict faced the developers: the creation of the new school dis-

23. Letter from Robert J. Gustafson, Monroe County Planning Council, to Mr. Samuel Jackson, Assistant Secretary for Community Planning and Management, HUD, Feb. 14, 1972.

trict. Their only obstacles to success after this were the capabilities of New Wayne Communities' management and future economic conditions.

Education: A Knotty Problem

Continuous success of the developers in gaining public acceptance of the project through 1970 and 1971 avoided controversy over the new-community concept. There is a difference between concept and detail; local reaction had not been tested when exposed to specific aspects of the project plan. The occasion for this confrontation loomed as the developers examined alternatives for achieving educational goals for the project.

Great emphasis was placed on the social objectives of the project, one of which was to create innovative approaches for comprehensive education opportunities. The Gananda site is located in two central school districts: Palmyra-Macedon School District (70 percent); and Wayne-Central School District (30 percent). Education in New York State is administered at the local level by elected boards of education and an appointed superintendent of schools. All the districts are authorized to operate elementary, and junior and senior high schools. Annual operating budgets and bond issues for new construction are approved by district residents. Thus, for the developers, the prospect of area residents voting for new schools in Gananda presented a source of conflict.[24]

As one of the few opportunities residents have for directly influencing property taxation, the school budget or bond vote allows voters to express their dissatisfaction with increased taxes. New Wayne Communities developed a strategy to contend with this critical juncture in the development process. Recognizing that the proposition of an innovative educational system for Gananda would be hard to achieve if divided between two school districts, and that the issue of increasing local taxes by expanded district population would be a controversial issue, the developers took two steps.[25] The first of these was to bring the two boards

24. During 1970–1972 a record percentage of school district budget and bond issues were defeated by New York State voters.
25. A detailed description of Rouse's method of creating an innovative educational system for Columbia, Maryland, can be found in Gurney Breckenfeld, *Columbia and the New Cities* (New York: Ives Washburn, 1971), pp. 298–301. The

and superintendents into their confidence by a full disclosure of plans. The atmosphere of an "executive session" and the New Wayne Communities' persuasive abilities secured promises of full cooperation from the districts. The second step was to retain an educational consultant.

Although occupancy of the first housing and community facilities was not planned until the fall of 1974, Moot did not want to face the potential obstacle of a school issue at the last minute. A new school building usually requires three years from presentation to the voters to completion of construction. His timetable was to have a consultant's report completed in the fall of 1971. The consultant's recommendations could be reviewed for action in 1972, school building plans could be completed in early 1973, and a building available for the first site occupants in 1974.

In October, 1971, the Educational Policy Research Center of Syracuse University Research Corporation presented its findings. The report concluded that

the dual and external loci of authority are problematic for Gananda for two reasons. First, authorities with different problems and perspectives might not accept the approach to education represented in this document which is intimately linked with other social and economic programs. Second, even if there were no disagreements about philosophy and approach, the division of authority could make planning and administration difficult and undermine other objectives. For example, in which school district a parcel of land lies might become the dominant criteria in locating an industry or choosing a home.

The consultants suggested several options for the resolution of these problems:

Several options with respect to the locus of legal authority and its relationship with Gananda are theoretically possible. The first was to leave matters as they stood and have the authority for the schools in Gananda split between the two existing districts. A second option was to consolidate the two districts so that Gananda schools would be controlled by a

---

problems faced by new-community developers building in rural areas are similar. An attractive feature of the comprehensive development approach is the ability to create new educational opportunities. However, sites in rural areas are affected by conservative, older voters who are not benefiting from the new school systems but are forced to support the change through increased taxes. Variations in state education laws require unique solutions to the educational needs, although basic strategies can be similar.

single source of authority. The third option was to attempt to make the territory of Gananda a separate district itself. A fourth possibility was to leave the boundaries of Palmyra-Macedon and Wayne Central districts as they stood but create Gananda as a special area with some autonomy through a Joint Policy Committee with members from each school board and from Gananda. A fifth option was to designate the area of Gananda as a special unit and grant to a publicly chartered corporation through contract with each of the districts the power to conduct the educational program.[26]

Moot and his staff reviewed these options to select an approach that did not compromise their planning objectives. They chose the route which offered the greatest source of potential conflict but the least amount of compromise: creating a new district. This extraordinary procedure, if successful, would remove the project from any future local objections having to do with educational matters.

In February and March of 1972, Moot and his consultants met in private with each board of education and superintendent. New Wayne Communities, represented by Paul Barru, gained the support of these groups for the campaign to win voter confidence. First public announcement of this approach was made in April, 1972. Superintendents of both the Palmyra-Macedon and Wayne-Central districts supported the proposal. Procedures involved in creating the new district required four steps: (1) approval of the proposal by the State Education Department; (2) passage of a special bill by the State Legislature; (3) signing of the bill by the Governor; and (4) approval of the existing districts to cede portions to the new district.

The school boards supported the proposal but insisted that four safeguards be written into the proposed legislation:

(1) A public referendum would be held in each district prior to creation of any new district.

(2) Gananda would continue to pay its proportionate share of existing indebtedness until the indebtedness be retired.

(3) Children presently residing in Gananda's area would be allowed to choose between attending new Gananda schools or schools in their former home districts. Gananda would be

26. Educational Policy Research Center, SURC, *Education in Gananda: A Statement of Philosophy and Framework* (Syracuse, N.Y., 1971).

required to pay tuition for those students who decided to attend the other schools.

(4) Present residents in the Gananda area would be protected from a higher tax burden than they would normally have if they remained in present school districts.

With the support of the boards of education and approval of the State Education Department, the "Gananda Education Bill" was passed by the State Assembly on May 3, 1972, and was promptly signed by the Governor. A date for the public referendum was set for November 27, 1972. The methods the developer used to present the proposal to the voters and the outcome provide insight into approaches for handling controversial subjects.

During the summer of 1972 community discussion about the issue raised questions as to the effect of the project on taxes for the area resident. Although New Wayne Communities had attempted to present their techniques to prevent this criticism, "Letters to the Editor" in the local papers in October cited this issue. One lifetime resident stated that "I don't trust developers' promises. Someone who lives in the District before the New Town can't get out of paying more taxes." By early November the developers were becoming apprehensive about voter rejection of the new school district. On November 14, 1972, less than two weeks before the vote, the developer held a press conference on the subject. It was announced that a new member of the staff would be assigned to concentrate on talking to Gananda area residents about the proposed new district. Lorraine Finley, who is the wife of the popular state assemblyman for the residents of the Gananda area, was introduced by Barru as the new special consultant for the vote. She was convinced of the merits of the project and worked diligently at her paid assignment.

On November 20, 1972, the developer held a public meeting for local district voters. The crowd was described as "skeptical" and unconvinced and dissatisfied with answers given by the New Wayne Communities representatives. One of the program's critics left the meeting unconvinced, stating: "They really didn't say anything. When they got through talking you weren't sure what question you asked. I still have a lot of questions." However, one of the questioners, with grandchildren living in the Gananda area, felt that most of her questions on taxes were answered to her satisfaction. The full impact of the new community on area school districts was explained at the meeting. It was estimated that by 1980 Gananda would have more students than the combined populations of the Palmyra-Macedon and Wayne-Central districts. In press releases immediately prior to the voting day Wayne-Central Superintendent William A. Crombe was quoted: "If we don't cede this territory we are going to be inundated."

Superintendent Carroll Hutt, of Palmyra-Macedon, reminded voters that both districts had to approve the proposal for it to pass: "It's pretty hard to predict what the impact will be, but if residents turn down the new school district it could mean we'd be voting every year on a new building referendum. . . . Palmyra-Macedon and Wayne could be faced with excessive overcrowding if the districts had to absorb all the students." [27]

Results of the vote held on November 27, 1972, were overwhelmingly in favor of the new district. Palmyra-Macedon voters approved the measure by a six-to-one majority; Wayne-Central residents voted ten-to-one. The developers had won their only public referendum. For the remainder of the project's future the only source of conflict for the project would be in the Joint Preliminary Review Board's individual project reviews. This would appear to present a picture of clear sailing for the developers; however, internal management problems opened opportunities for the greatest amount of criticism the project would receive.

Management Problems

The ability of Moot and his management team to gain local acceptance and avoid conflict remained constant over the first four years of the project. As the project moved from planning into development of details, flaws started to show; the management's inexperience in large-scale development began to worry shareholders.

On September 11, 1972, Gananda shareholders approved a new roster of top management. Moot was removed as chief executive but retained his seat on the board of directors. It became apparent that the controlling interests of the family of the Xerox

27. *Palmyra Courier Journal*, Nov. 22, 1972.

founder, Jerome Wilson, influenced the changes. In March of 1973, local newspapers announced the appointment of a new chief officer for New Wayne Communities. William E. Norcross headed a management consultant firm, Wenco, Inc., which had developed several large real estate development projects for the Wilson family. Norcross' assignment was to assemble a staff capable of carrying out the development and to act as project manager for Gananda.

The announcement for management changes came at a critical time for the project. Initial detailed plans were to go before the Joint Preliminary Review Board for review and approval in early 1973. Without continued favorable support the project could be aborted. On January 26, New Wayne Communities announced that 440 housing units of Phase I would be submitted to the board. Several articles and Letters to the Editor critical of the project management's ability to meet commitments surfaced. Reflecting on the problems of Reston, Virginia, Monroe County Planner Don B. Martin pointed out that the burden of development costs could end the idealism shown by the developers: "The developers end up compromising to make ends meet. They get impatient and become unwilling to take risks." With the advent of a new management team, the question arose of whether the profit motive had replaced idealism at Gananda.

On the critical presentation date of March 9, Moot and Norcross faced this issue. Speaking candidly, Moot admitted that from the beginning of the project he had informed shareholders that he did not want to be in corporate management in the construction: "My background is just not there."[28] Conceding the vagueness of details, Moot stated that largely because of HUD requirements "we did not really accomplish what we should have in development and communication with planning boards. Let's start having a good open rapport because that is the way we want to operate."[29]

One of the key strategies for obtaining local support—using broad concepts with little definition—was now starting to backfire on the developers. Local criticism from the towns and county board of supervisors reprimanded the company for the proce-

28. *Rochester Times-Union*, Oct. 2, 1973.
29. *Rochester Democrat and Chronicle*, March 10, 1973.

dures used.[30] New Wayne Communities needed local approval of 440 units of housing, a park system, and a sewage treatment plant. Supervisor Marvin stated that: "I think it is high time the Gananda people get down here and give up what priorities there are as far as Gananda is concerned."

On July 1, a new management team for the project was announced by Norcross, and Paul Brady took over the difficult task of convincing critics of the stability of the project and its capability to meet commitments. Local newspapers carried articles describing Brady's experience and listed the local shareholders who retained control of the company. Continuity of the concept for the project was emphasized to dispel doubts of local officials who were wondering whether promises made by departed officers carried any weight. Accessibility of local officials to the new officers, favorable and extensive press coverage, and an atmosphere of candor, seemed to lessen controversy over the project. Gananda officials repeated that no ideals had changed, describing management shifts as appropriate for the change from a planning stage to a construction stage. One of the chief officers stated that "we're going to make mistakes. We know that. We will attempt to minimize mistakes by good planning. We think we have the management and inhouse staff to provide good planning in all areas."[31]

The twenty-five investors who put up more than $1 million held firm. A lengthy four-part article in the *Rochester Times-Union* in October, 1973, provided details of their continued support, naming all individuals and placing local prestige behind the project. This support, and public disclosure, contributed to the approvals secured for the necessary components of Phase I of construction.

Summary

Unlike the single major event of a public hearing at Lysander, the Gananda project was subject to a series of events with potential for community conflict. This contrast can be attributed to the risks that Stewart Moot took when he created a Joint Preliminary

30. Two headlines stated: "Moot Admits Lack of Contact with Planners" (*Democrat and Chronicle*, March 10, 1973), and "Palmyra, Macedon Supervisors Criticize Gananda Procedures" (*Palmyra Courier-Journal*, May 30, 1973).
31. *Rochester Times-Union*, Oct. 2, 1973.

Review Board. By relying on candid disclosure of the new-community plans and procedures for development, Moot gained early acceptance of the New Wayne Communities project. His strategy of presenting broad concepts supported with a little detail also assisted in diminishing the potential for controversy at the start of the project. Later, however, this strategy provided negative results as public officials requested more details. The management team's inability to satisfactorily respond to requests for details on the project, and dissatisfaction of the shareholders with management's abilities, caused local officials to raise doubts about the project. This was translated into resistance to the new project, reflecting conflict between the developer and the community.

In contrast to Lysander, then, Gananda presented an ongoing process of potential conflicts. Events related to the central issues of: (1) the developer's leadership; (2) the nature or source of the proposal; and (3) the method of proposal presentation to the public are summarized as follows.

Leadership of the Developer. The most direct test of a leader's personality is the way a project is identified. If Gananda was readily labeled as "Moot's project," then clearly it could be said that Moot had qualities that contributed to the project's ready acceptance. However, this was not the case. When questioned, local residents had difficulty recalling Moot's name or his involvement in the project. The project became identified with the "nice people," as one former landowner said, who came out to talk with him about buying his land. The "nice people" was a general description for the management team and staff that Moot assembled at the beginning of the project.

It has been difficult to determine whether Moot's early staff selections were intentionally directed to members of the clergy or if this is only the cynic's point of view. It is more likely that Moot interviewed and selected staff whose attitudes reflected his interests. These selections were appropriate for translating Moot's desires for social innovations to meet human needs. Community acceptance of the project and the minimal controversy surrounding its early phase can be attributed more to an atmosphere created by Gananda staff than to Moot's personality. Robinson Lapp, Paul Barru, and Lorraine Finley are remembered for their sincerity and candor. Staff members and local supporters of

Gananda did not follow Stewart Moot, the person, but the concept of a new community. For employees it was an exciting job, and for investors a moderate-risk speculative investment.

Stewart Moot is a soft-spoken bespectacled man with a kindly smile. Whether in public or in private, he answers questions in a quiet reserved way. His mood and style elicit a genuine sense of honesty and warmth. These characteristics were reflected in the key staff members designated with responsibility for public contacts. In a sense, Moot did personalize the Gananda organization with his character. It was more one of anonymity than individualism. The "nice people" sobriquet was fitting for the management of New Wayne Communities.

It is interesting to note that as the key staff changes occurred, and Moot was replaced in the public eye by Norcross and others, public criticism of the project occurred more frequently than before. This change can be attributed, at least in part, to doubts in the community created by a businesslike and somewhat detached new management team.

The ongoing nature of the project after a complete staff turnover in 1972, and Moot's diminishing role from 1972 on, illustrate the independence of the concept from the initiator. The stability of the project now rests in the corporate form of organization sustained by the shareholders.

Nature or Source of Proposal. Events during the Gananda proposal phase illustrate the effect that changing leadership can have on public attitudes. It appears that the corporate structure of a privately sponsored development project, through personnel changes, can vary not only its leadership but the personality of its organization.

Comparing Lysander and Gananda in the aspect of management changes, we find that Lysander diminished controversy by this move, whereas Gananda increased controversy. The strength of Gananda as a privately sponsored project was in the respect held for the local financial supporters. The controlling interests of several of Rochester's leading industries were represented on the Gananda board of directors, a factor which influenced local acceptance of the project.

Method of Proposal Presentation to Public. Gananda's early management team labored long and hard to obtain the support of the landowners and public officials in the area. Management's subtle yet direct personal approach to individuals and groups was a successful strategy. An atmosphere of credibility and a desire to want to believe people like Lapp and Barru dispelled any potential controversy.

Unlike other massive land assemblies, such as that for Columbia, Maryland, Moot's work was done openly without attempts at deception or subterfuge. By moving rapidly in gaining support of leading figures, such as the towns' supervisors, Moot gained invaluable advocates for the project. Property owners on the site who were accustomed to consulting local Supervisors Hack or Marvin for advice, were convinced that Gananda was good for them and for their communities. Several speculators tried to enter the area to purchase key parcels before Moot had finished his buying, but they were unsuccessful. Their failure has been attributed to the people's belief in Moot and his staff and their suspicion of other developers.

Moot's most trying times for potential controversy developed as he was being pressed for detailed explanations of broad conceptual plans. The announcement of Title VII designation as the tenth federally assisted new town dispelled this controversy, for a while.

If one were to graph the sequence of events (Figure 4.3) for Gananda in relation to presentation of the proposal there would be two separate lines. The first represents the constant factor of

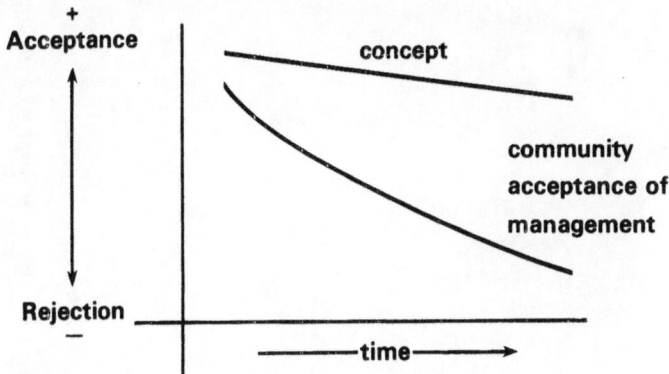

Figure 4.3. Gananda: Sequence of events during the proposal phase

the concept itself. New Wayne Communities' adherence to social innovations and local support for the credibility of Moot and his staff remained relatively unchanged. The second line represents community acceptance of the project management. This line moves negatively over time, as local demand for project details and management revisions affect public attitudes. The idea sustained itself, but confidence in management's ability to execute waned.

The public demand for details did not affect Lysander in the same way as Gananda. This and other critical factors will be examined in our third case study in the following chapter.

5 | Riverton

Our third case study is Riverton, a planned new community located in the town of Henrietta, nine miles south of Rochester along the New York State Thruway (Figure 5.1). It was the seventh development to receive a loan guarantee under provisions of Title VII of the 1970 Housing Act. The eventual population figure is projected to be about 25,000 for a development located on approximately 2,500 acres.

The story of the planning phase of Riverton is closely tied to the background of Robert E. Simon and his experience in developing Reston, Virginia. Simon, who was president of Riverton Properties, Inc., during the period covered by this study, has strong opinions about the development of new communities. This characteristic and his personal experiences with Reston influenced events for Riverton.

Events occurring in the town of Henrietta, before and during Riverton's development, illustrate the effect of actions by elected officials and public employees on a large-scale development. A developer who has aroused little public opposition and has gained the confidence of local officials during the proposal stage probably will have faced no more than one or two public debates, and other opportunities for controversy will not have surfaced.[1] However, a subtle and devastating form of conflict occurs

1. This is the general model of controversy being "dependent on previous events in a community," as described by James S. Coleman in *Community Conflict* (New York: The Free Press, 1957), p. 7.

Figure 5.1. Map of Riverton and environs

when officials and public employees are not in agreement with a project and make covert and indirect efforts to prevent development. In effect, a new-community builder must become a "partner" with local government, depending on local government to cooperate in the provision of public services and the community infrastructure. This cooperation can range from investment in new facilities to an endorsement of the developer's plans. Under any arrangement, the developer must be prepared to show the public how the proposed development will have an impact on the individual and the community.

This chapter describes the events surrounding the Riverton project in the town of Henrietta from 1968 to 1973. Particular emphasis is given to the process of government review during this period.

Project Background

This history of the Riverton project begins with the optioning of farmland by a Rochester developer, Milton Karz, in 1968. His previous experience in the early 1960's had been with a suburban apartment development known as College Complex. Located across from the entrance to Monroe County Community College, it has grown steadily to over 1,000 units. Karz, looking for additional development opportunities, considered a site to the south to have attractive potential. He assembled land on both sides of the New York State Thruway in the town of Henrietta and proposed a planned unit development that was at first called Genesee Village.

The town of Henrietta was growing rapidly and had increased from 11,000 to 35,000 in just ten years.[2] Employment in the region had been spurred by expansion in the two major industries: manufacturing and education. Corporations such as Kodak, Xerox, and Bausch and Lomb had grown tremendously in the 1960's. A diverse array of educational institutions—the University of Rochester, the Rochester Institute of Technology, and a collection of smaller colleges and specialized institutions—experienced major enrollment gains and built new facilities during the same period.

The Genesee Village site included thirteen major landholdings and was located at the edge of the expanding Rochester urbanized area. Land costs reached a high of $6,000 per acre adjacent to the Thruway; land to the south ran considerably less, averaging $2,800 per acre. After securing control by purchase of approximately 10 percent of the site, as well as holdings and options or purchase contracts for all but a small part of the contiguous area, Karz examined the site-development potential in detail. A preliminary market study supported the development

2. *U.S. Census of Population*, 1970. Overall county growth was 20.5 percent, second highest in New York State. The town of Henrietta is directly in the path of the southern-expansion pattern of Monroe County.

because of its accessibility, proximity to major employment centers, and readily available utilities.[3] A report prepared for the Urban Development Corporation (UDC) considered the site one of the three primary new-community locations in the region,[4] citing it as being "situated in an area which affords great opportunity for expansion."

Karz decided in mid-1970 to seek rezoning for part of the site from single-family residential to apartment use. This would allow for the first stage of a large development that would eventually include shopping and industrial areas. Strong opposition to rezoning the land developed from an adjacent homeowner's association, protesting (1) rising taxes; (2) increasing traffic congestion; and (3) lowered property values.

These comments were offered in Letters to the Editor and articles in the regional editions of the local Rochester newspapers. The general tone of the remarks was similar to that of a homeowner adjacent to the Genesee Village site, who said that "more apartments will ruin the town for us. We moved out of the City [Rochester] just to get away from them and the politicians let the big developers in."[5]

The zoning hearing was well attended. Repeated expressions of anger were aimed at the town board for permissive zoning and the ease of obtaining variances to the ordinance. Typical comments indicated concern for the rapid growth of the town, excessive apartment construction, and increasing taxes.[6] The recently formed Citizens for Better Henrietta was represented by their secretary, Frank Mancini. He commented:

We left the City of Rochester as we liked to live in suburban surroundings, and away from the noise and the smell, the traffic and the confragration (sic), the pollution and the smog. Henrietta gives us all the reverse, green hills and plains, sunshine, valley and quiet. You want to destroy what we hold sacred, our peace of mind and our right to live in peace and enjoy what we produce with our toils. What you are about to do, if you will do it, is destroy what is left of Henrietta as a suburban

3. Real Estate Research Corporation, *Development Analysis: Henrietta and Wheatland Properties* (Jan. 1965).

4. Rochester Center for Governmental and Community Research, *Planned Communities for the Rochester Metropolitan Area* (March, 1970).

5. Robert McClelland, quoted in the *Rochester Times-Union*, Feb. 17, 1971.

6. Town of Henrietta Hearing (Minutes of Meeting, May 20, 1970).

town. Beware you will be punished by the voters when your day comes.[7]

At that moment the project seemed finished. However, Karz looked for ways to preserve his investments and sought to interest others.[8] He was eventually able to persuade Stanndco (a local home-building firm with strong roots in Henrietta), Howard Samuels (former undersecretary of commerce, president and chairman of the New York City Off-Track Betting Commission), and most significantly Robert E. Simon (founder of Reston), to join with him to move the project forward.

The new management team selected by Simon, to oversee the Riverton (formerly Genesee Village) project established goals in order to achieve construction start by the summer of 1972, less than three years away. Four major steps were outlined:

(1) Adoption by the town of Henrietta of a Planned Unit Development (PUD) ordinance.[9]

(2) Approval of the Riverton application for a PUD ordinance.

(3) Submission of application for HUD Title VII financial assistance.

(4) Approval of final plan for Riverton.

The scope of the project (aiming for a population of 25,600 on 2,560 acres in sixteen years) left the new owners confident in their chances for success in meeting these goals. However, much of the work of gaining local acceptance would fall on the principals of the new organization.

7. *The Henrietta Post*, Oct. 1, 1970.

8. Out-of-pocket expenditures at that time were probably not much more than $50,000 for options and preliminary planning. By early 1972 they had reached $1.5 million. From the unpublished report on Riverton by John Stainton, Riverton Staff Technical Director (Mimeographed; March, 1972).

9. The Planned Unit Development (PUD) is a device used in zoning ordinances to allow an entire area plan to be submitted for approval, subject to standards of regulation which are applied at the time of approval rather than being preset in the ordinance. This concept allows unified developments for residential, commercial, industrial, or mixed-use purposes to be reviewed at the time of submission. The principle is well suited for new-community planning because of the emphasis on procedural requirements rather than specific land-use criteria. See International City Managers Association, *Principles and Practices of Urban Planning* (Washington, D.C., 1968), pp. 480–484; Charles M. Haar, *Land-Use Planning*, 2d ed. (Boston: Little, Brown, 1971), pp. 191–196; Daniel R. Mandelker, *Managing Our Urban Environment* (New York: Bobbs-Merrill, 1963), pp. 823–838.

Robert E. Simon and the Management Team

Karz was immediately put in the background by the new management team. The Stanndco firm was spoken of in the local press as a "homebuilder of quality subdivisions." Emphasis was placed on the pleasant atmosphere created by Stanndco in their developments, and an identification with Stanndco, as symbolic of high standards, was carried forward in press releases. Stanndco had built in Henrietta and adjacent Monroe County towns with a reputation for pleasant residential environments, although Stanndco's public-relations image was not supported by some project neighbors.

Howard Samuels' local identification is important in understanding the shift of attention away from Karz. Samuels is from the Rochester area; he was a successful businessman before entering public life, and the media has treated him favorably in his public career. As a young man he started a small operation for the manufacture of plastic products in the adjacent Wayne County village of Macedon. His invention of "Kordite" expanded into a manufacturing entity eventually acquired by Mobil Oil Company in the early 1960's. Finding himself a retired millionaire at 40, Samuels turned to politics and to investing in real estate. Riverton was brought to his attention, and he decided to participate in the project.

While Samuels' involvement contributed to local support of the project, Robert Simon's connection was even more useful; his presence was capitalized on to the fullest extent possible. Simon was described as Riverton's "man-in-motion"; his photographs were prominent in the local newspapers. An identification was developed between Simon's objectives as a developer, his new town of Reston, and Riverton. A typical headline read: "Simon's Aim: Solve Suburban Sprawl."

Simon was elected president of Riverton Properties in 1969 and quickly became the principal force in shaping the direction of the next stages of work. By Simon's influence the project was converted in local eyes from a subdivision by Karz to an exciting new town. At one point, local officials from the town and the regional planning board were flown to Reston for a tour of the new town. The benefits of this trip were shown by the convincing observation of the school board president, who said: "I think that Reston is a livable place. A lot of thought has been given to the way land can be used by people and not destroyed by them. I think this sort of planning is something that should have started 20 years ago in Henrietta."[10]

A three-part article in the Rochester newspapers described Reston and was introduced by a brief paragraph saying that "Robert E. Simon, the president of Reston, created Reston, the nation's first new town." The result was inevitable: Riverton-Reston became the image of the new project. Simon, the creator of Reston, was the "man behind Riverton."

Simon is a persuasive individual, capable of gaining support through his sincerity and expression of honest interest in whomever and whatever he is involved. For example, in a newspaper editorial recommending that the town board support the project, confidence in Simon was described this way:

Robert Simon, chief planner of the project, has shown in the much-praised Reston development near Washington, that he does not compromise on esthetics or construction quality. If his backers will commit themselves to fully carry out plans presented to the town, one can have confidence that Henrietta will get an outstanding asset.[11]

Simon firmly believed that the chief executive of a new community must take the responsibility for working out a guiding philosophy for its plan. He believed that new-community development was intended

for people who live and work in the community to have the widest possible opportunity to use their full potential of mind and body; for it to be possible for any who want to stay in this one community to do so throughout their lives; and for the importance of each individual to be considered over the importance of the community.[12]

His Reston experiences left him realistic about the problems of new-town development. He was aware that "a new community is planning, but the object of the planning exercise is, after all, to build. Without good political relationships there might be planning, but there cannot be building."[13] To carry forward the

10. Rush-Henrietta School PTA Meeting, Nov. 17, 1970.
11. *Henrietta Post*, Oct. 1, 1970.
12. Robert E. Simon, "The Challenge of Starting New Communities," *HUD Challenge* (Washington, D.C., Aug., 1972).
13. *Ibid.*

building of Riverton Simon put together a local staff that was headed by Andrew Goldman, an attorney, who was appointed executive vice-president. Goldman previously served as area director and acting regional counsel for the State Urban Development Corporation and was associate counsel for the New York City Housing and Regional Development Board. The task of creating a development organization, and gaining approval of the Riverton proposal through the local planning and governmental framework, was begun. Two simultaneous efforts were put forward: (1) local approval of the project; and (2) selection by HUD for Title VII financial assistance.

Project Development

The sprawl that characterizes metropolitan suburbs is particularly noticeable in Henrietta. The land is relatively flat, and much of it has remained in active farm use. Tree cover is usually found only in wet untillable areas. The town is one of the less prestigious Rochester suburbs and has developed rapidly with low-price tract homes, garden apartments, and extensive areas for light industrial and warehouse use. Zoning of commercial land has followed market pressures, with strips of development extending outward for many miles along the most heavily traveled roads.

Planning and land-use controls had been relatively weak up to 1969. Except for the city of Rochester, only one of the nineteen local town and village planning boards within the county had professional staffs. Much of what passed for planning at the local town level had simply been a response of market forces to real estate tax considerations. With rapidly rising school costs (and consequent higher taxes), developers were having an increasingly hard time obtaining local approval for new projects. One result, either consciously or unconsciously, had been to raise development standards (which should not be confused with effective land-use planning) and to impose various entrance fees on developers and new residents.

Within this framework, planning a new community to include a mixture of housing types, community facilities, commercial and industrial uses has to be a long, difficult, and expensive process. In Riverton the local town board, used to dealing with the details of specific subdivision tracts and individual industrial and commercial development proposals, was suddenly faced with a proposal of massive size and complexity to be carried out over an extended period of time. Repeatedly, in public discussions the feeling was expressed that a professional planner was needed to assist the town board in deliberating the issues, for the total impact to be expected on roads, utilities, schools, and other facilities soon became apparent.

Riverton carried out its development program under controls specified in the town of Henrietta's Planned Unit Development Ordinance (PUD). The ordinance is based on a model prepared by the Monroe County Planning Council staff and a local nonprofit organization, the Rochester Center for Governmental and Community Research. The ordinance provides for greatly increased flexibility in the mixture of uses and allows for the clustering of buildings to increase the community open spaces. A minimum development of 300 contiguous acres is required for a proposal to qualify under the ordinance.

The group opposing the Genesee Village project, the Citizens for Better Henrietta, was organized in early 1970. The form of opposition taken by this group was similar to that followed by the Homeowners' Association in Baldwinsville. Quickly organized, the group appeared at the public hearing on the PUD ordinance in June, 1970, to express disagreement with the proposal for development in Henrietta. The general impression was of a group of dissidents, typical of those who appear at zoning hearings to oppose any form of development that disrupts the local setting.[14] They were ineffective as opposition, and the ordinance was adopted by the Board in July, 1970.

Approvals under the ordinance proceed in a multiple-step process starting with preparation by the developer of a sketch master plan, a public hearing, approval of the master plan by the town board, then submission of a preliminary and final site plan for each two-year stage of development to the town planning board. Although greater flexibility may ultimately be achieved, following the timetable for approvals under the PUD ordinance can add considerably to the cost of doing business. The schedule projected for Riverton was indicative of the lead time frequently necessary before construction starts (see Table 5.1). The town board

14. General comments were addressed at three concerns: (1) increased taxes; (2) disruption of rural atmosphere; and (3) losses in property values.

Table 5.1. Time schedule for zoning approvals for Riverton

Date	Requests for approval
May, 1970	Public hearing on PUD ordinance
July, 1970	Passage of PUD ordinance
July, 1970	Submission of Riverton master plan to town board
April, 1971	Approval of master plan by planning board
May, 1971	Public hearing on master plan
July, 1971	Approval of master plan by town board
Sept., 1971	Submission of preliminary first stage two-year plan to planning board (502 units, plus industrial)
March, 1972	Approval of preliminary plan by planning board
March, 1972	Submission of final plan to planning board
March, 1972	Approval of final plan by planning board
April, 1972	Start of construction

delayed action on the approval of preliminary planning until June and offset the construction start to September. This was too late in the season to begin site work, and the developers had to wait until the spring of 1973. The exasperating delays by local agencies during the course of the proposal phase prompted editorial notice in the local papers and demands for action on several occasions. For example, one editorial stated [15] that "the time is at hand when the board must move on the Riverton project, or possibly lose the opportunity of having a highly desirable project built in Henrietta."

Almost two years later, the Henrietta Chamber of Commerce launched a study to find out what's "bogging down the Riverton project." [16] Each step of the development process involved extensive reviews by various public agencies and lay boards, often in greater detail than for other builders because of the project's ultimate size. It was up to the developer to keep the agencies (sometimes within the same level of government) informed and coordinated. The process was complicated by three changes of administration in town government, as well as by the abolishment, then later re-establishment, of the town planning board.

Among the agencies and organizations involved in the local approval process were the town board, town planning board,

15. *Henrietta Post*, Oct. 1, 1970.   16. *Rochester Times-Union*, Jan. 10, 1972.

Rush-Henrietta School District, Henrietta Volunteer Fire Department, town Public Works Department, town engineer, town consulting engineer for sewerage, town consulting engineer for water, town building inspector, Monroe County Planning Council, Monroe County Public Works Department, Monroe County Pure Water Authority, Monroe County Health Department, New York State Soil Conservation Service, and New York State Department of Transportation.

Parallel to—and independent of—the zoning process, were the submissions and planning reviews carried out as part of the developers' decision to seek a federal loan guarantee for $12,000,000 under Title VII of the Housing Act of 1970. The decision was made for a variety of reasons.[17] The most obvious one is to obtain the federal insurance that makes it possible to finance the cost of land purchase and site development at a lower interest rate. However, the costs of preparing and processing these applications have in most cases offset the interest saved. Potentially more significant is the priority for grant funds (in most cases applied for through the local community) for sewer, water, and other basic development expenses; priority for federally insured subsidized housing programs; and priority for other grants for such diverse uses as hospitals and highways. In addition to these basic grants, the HUD New Communities Office is authorized to supplement these funds by 20 percent of the total project cost.[18]

A third reason for seeking federal guarantees is less easily quantified, and at this point can be only speculative. The guarantee may serve to increase investor and perhaps resident confidence in the long-range financial stability and soundness of the

---

17. The two most important features were the availability of public service and supplementary grants. Both grants ease the burden of expense for the developer and the existing community during the initial start-up period. Services and facilities can be made available to provide a more attractive community to potential residents at the outset. See Hugh Mields, Jr., *Federally Assisted New Communities* (Washington, D.C.: Urban Land Institute, 1973), pp. 32–38.

18. Title VII of the 1970 Housing Act provided opportunities for new communities to obtain supplementary grants in conjunction with 13 federal programs, including mass transportation, highways, airports, public health facilities, libraries, recreation and open-space lands, and neighborhood facilities. See HUD, Office of New Communities Development, *Outline of New Communities Assistance Programs* (Washington, D.C., Jan., 1971).

development. This confidence could reasonably increase the rate of development, which would further reinforce the chances for success.

A fourth reason—and perhaps the real basis for much of the enthusiasm—is the relatively low equity requirement under the Title VII program. The principals of a new-community project would be able to undertake an extensive development program with financing that would not cause them to lose control of the project.

Control, however, in the traditional sense for land development, means maintaining a majority interest in the financial aspect of the project.[19] New communities introduce another factor of control, and that is: the influence of elected officials and public employees on the future of the project. Each "partnership" that is formed with a local government or public agency for obtaining grants directly assisting a project exposes the developer to a compromise in the control of the project. Both Robert Simon and James Rouse were faced with this prospect in creating Reston and Columbia. Some of Rouse's adventures in placating bureaucracies and still keeping his development costs in line are humorous. In one case, the damming of a river to create a lake was so burdened by Corps of Engineers' requirements that projected costs reached $900,000. By creating a lake through ingenious engineering elsewhere on the site and ignoring the Corps, Rouse completed the lake for $250,000.

Processing through the HUD New Communities Office involves extensive reviews completely separate from local zoning procedures. Not only does the New Communities Office itself go over the material in detail, but, as with all federally supported programs, regional, state, and federal agencies become involved both through the A-95 review established by the federal Office of Management and Budget and through the review required by the Environmental Impact Statement.[20]

19. A general discussion of the subject can be found in Philip David, *Urban Land Development* (Homewood, Ill.: Richard D. Irwin, Inc., 1970). The financial and management problems are discussed in two papers by Mahlon Apgar, IV, "New Business from New Towns?" in *Harvard Business Review* (Jan.–Feb., 1971); and *Managing Community Development* (New York: McKinsey, 1971).

20. The Genesee-Finger Lakes Regional Planning Board, covering an eight-county area is the designated "local clearing-house." In practice, clearance at least

The chances for delay and the need for frequent adjustments in plans to satisfy various local, state, and federal agencies are obvious. John Stainton, responsible for the technical development of the project, has criticized the process for its obstacles to the private developer.

It should also be obvious that proper sequencing of both privately constructed development and needed community facilities is extremely difficult under the present circumstances. Indeed, the federal New Communities Program, designed to promote more effective land development patterns and reduce the initial risk and uncertainties associated with such development may possibly even be counterproductive as it appears to have substantially increased the cost and risks for those who choose the federal route.[21]

A major series of events involving local review occurred in successive steps after passage of the PUD ordinance. A parallel set of important events occurred as part of the A-95 review process prior to submission for Title VII New Communities assistance. Both sets of events were bound closely to the development of a master plan, slated for local presentation in May, 1971, which would then be submitted as part of the Title VII application in the fall of 1971.

Master Plan Development

Riverton Properties set up a tentative timetable of twelve months from the passage of the PUD ordinance to the approval of the Riverton application for a planned unit development. By spring 1971 the architectural and planning firm of Rogers, Taliaferro, Kostritsky, and Lamb (RTKL) of Baltimore was to have prepared a suitable master plan for the controlled 1,500 acres for public presentation. There were major constraints in the site's characteristics. The land was shaped largely by glacial action, which left the area a series of gently rolling hills with a number of clearly defined drumlins. Only a few slopes are over 10 percent in grade. Except for a few poorly drained areas, nearly all of the land has been actively farmed for many years.

---

in the Rochester area has meant approval. Thus, the board is in a key position to influence planning decisions and project approvals.

21. From the unpublished report by John Stainton, Riverton Staff Technical Director (Mimeographed; March, 1972).

Approximately 15 percent of the land, including some of the richest farmland, falls within the Genesee River flood plain. The river itself flows swiftly to the north, meets the New York State Barge Canal, and continues on to Rochester, and, over several major waterfalls, to Lake Ontario. The steep banks, ten to fifteen feet high except during the periods of high runoff, make it difficult to reach the water.

By the late 1960's existing improvements consisted of scattered farms and a number of paved roads, but the first signs of suburban development had begun to appear. A row of ranch-style houses had been built along the main north-south road; and Eagle Ridge, a small subdivision, was located a mile to the east.

Water lines run through the Riverton site but are of insufficient capacity to provide service. New mains would have to be built from a location a mile to the east. An existing major trunk sewer a mile to the south would have to be extended to provide initial service. A single track line of the Erie Railroad cuts diagonally across the site and provides the potential for rail access to the industrial land and an eventual rapid transit link to the City.

The First Master Plan. [22] Large-scale land planning tends, at least in this country, to show relatively little innovation. Riverton plans are no exception. Much of what would be considered innovation shows up only as detailed sub-area plans are developed. Of more significance, however, are the financing constraints on infrastructure development. New communities in this country are essentially a private effort, dependent ultimately on making a profit. In contrast, new-town development in Great Britain and Scandinavia has been initiated by public investment in land acquisition, planning, construction of public utilities and services, and providing financial assistance for private builders. It is generally not feasible for a developer to carry through plans that depend on a high level of costly infrastructure development. Under today's rules of the game, it would be foolhardy for the developer of a community like Riverton to prepare a plan that was dependent, for example, on any form of public transportation, on a large proportion of high-density housing, or on a technologically advanced form of community-wide heating or waste disposal.

22. Much of the following material is obtained from John Stainton's report, *ibid.*

Many master plans for communities the size of Riverton and larger have attempted to define a hierarchy of neighborhoods and villages which make up an overall "town" or "city." This is the pattern used for example at Columbia and Reston and more recently at Jonathan, in Minnesota.[23] Land planning then relates residential development to small neighborhood retail shops, elementary schools, and recreation facilities; these in turn relate to a larger village center, and the villages to the city center and regional shopping. While this pattern is followed to some extent in Riverton, it was felt to have limited importance. The plan was influenced more by site conditions, market and financial constraints, and the location of existing roads and utilities, than by any specific concern for creating a structural hierarchy.

The first Riverton plan was prepared by an architectural and planning firm and was largely guided by direct inputs from Robert Simon. As at Reston, Simon was motivated by the desire to develop a strong sense of community identification by creating a place where people could become easily acquainted with one another and where an array of conveniently located community services would give both children and adults the opportunity to live a full and meaningful life.[24] To Simon, this meant detailed attention to achieving an urban environment with: (1) housing planned at relatively high densities (or to state it another way, a limited number of detached single-family houses); (2) extensive walkways and open-space areas owned in common; (3) early provision of community buildings and recreation facilities; and (4) a full complement of educational, cultural, and health services located in or near Riverton to be operated by existing institutions

23. For comparative data on Title VII new communities, see Hugh Mields, Jr., *Federally Assisted New Communities*.

24. "Project Goals and Objectives" were outlined in *The Proposed Riverton New Community, Monroe County, Environmental Impact Statement* (Final draft; Riverton Properties, Inc., Nov. 19, 1971), p. 6: "To create a community where there will be optimal opportunity for interpersonal relations; to maximize the opportunities for people of different ages, races, and economic status to relate to each other by providing a wide range of housing types and prices within each neighborhood; to create opportunities for the fruitful and enjoyable use of free time by providing at all stages of development a variety of recreational, educational, and cultural facilities; to make it possible for those wanting to live and work in the same community to do so through provision of a broad employment base; to make Riverton a safer place for people of all ages through the separation of pedestrian and vehicular traffic to the maximum extent feasible."

within the metropolitan area. He was particularly interested in the development of a mixed-use area, Riverton Center, within which would be located a diverse range of activities. In addition to community-oriented retail functions, plans for the Center included a substantial residential population, offices, educational and entertainment facilities.

Additional objectives for Riverton, traditional to much of the new-town literature, were to provide: (1) a wide range of housing types both for rent and for sale; (2) nearby employment opportunities; (3) a separation of pedestrian and vehicular traffic by provision of a walkway system and underpasses; (4) a high level of architectural design and landscaping; and (5) careful site planning in respect to existing land forms and natural features.

In broad terms, the first plan identified most of these ideas, although the concept of mixed housing types would have to wait for more detailed planning. The first plan was submitted along with other supporting information to the town board for master plan approval; it also formed the basis of the initial HUD submission. The plan included:

	Gross area in acres	Percent of total acreage
Residential use	724	56
Commercial/mixed use	36	3
Industrial use	300	22
Public and community use	240	19
Total	1,300	100

Industrial areas were located along Thruway frontage, highly visible from the highway, and in a second area of fragmented landholdings and poor soil conditions at the eastern edge of the site. The latter was clearly considered "left over" and was for the most part to be held for later stages of development.

Significantly, the flood plain was shown to be developed in its entirety for residential use. A proposed golf course was located on upland portions of the site. There were several reasons why this course of action was chosen. A new dam had been constructed upstream in 1968, and no subsequent flooding had occurred in the area. With minor regrading, it was believed that the 100-year flood level was safe for building. An upland location for the golf course would maximize the value of residential frontage adjacent to the course, and would add to the sense of open space within the community itself. Economic factors, however, as well as strong objections from various public agencies, made it necessary to eliminate any proposals for residential construction within the flood plain. Residential building on the flood plain was criticized by the reviewing agencies in the A-95 process, as well as in the local press. The Citizens for Better Henrietta focused on this issue at every gathering where the Riverton representatives appeared.

In reconsidering their plans, Riverton's designers had to face the fact that loss of the flood-plain area for development would reduce the total buildable area. Local resistance to residential building on the flood plain was not so great as to prevent Riverton Properties from gaining approval from the town board, but the determined opposition of state and federal agencies to this aspect of the scheme eventually caused the developers to revise plans and acquire an additional 825 acres. To nullify the conflict the developers spent over $2 million on land purchases to expand the project. In 1972 storm Agnes caused flooding to the 100-year flood level along the Genesee River. No damage was done, but it served to reinforce the decision not to attempt any building within the flood-plain area.

Several of the plan's amenities for recreation and open space were considered vital for a satisfactory project. Their importance was emphasized by Simon, Goldman, and other representatives in public contacts. However, since the creation of community facilities was to be developed with state and federal support, the concurrence of representative agencies was necessary, entailing a process of negotiation that cost the developers unanticipated delays and expenses. One of the developers' representatives accused the town board of "taking maximum time allowed under the ordinance before approving each phase."

Whether to build a golf course at all was the subject of recurring discussion. Arguments were made that it took up too much of the open space, that it would be used by relatively few people in comparison to other uses, and that it was expensive to build. The developers finally concluded that the course would add an attractive landscaped element to the existing open site, enhance the marketability of the overall community, and provide an element that would encourage support from officials.

Other elements of the master plan are the walkways, the major road system, and the location of schools and retail facilities. The road system was taken from county and state master plan studies with only minor modifications after testing by a transportation consultant. School sites were located centrally to the population to be served in order to minimize or eliminate the need for busing. The plan anticipated 750 children for each elementary school, in accordance with current Henrietta school policy, and sizes of the sites were in conformance with state standards requiring 15 acres each. A site was also selected for a junior or senior high school, with the ultimate decision left to the school board.

Subsequent planning with school officials indicated the potential for development of more innovative school programs, including the location of specialized facilities within the Riverton Center complex and at other scattered locations, as well as the programming of a variety of community activities within the school buildings.

Additional community uses were anticipated for areas designated as "activity centers," which might include additional schools, neighborhood retail uses, indoor recreational facilities, space for community meetings, and day-care centers.

The amount of retail space was based upon market projections. The off-center location for Riverton Center was chosen over several alternative interior sites because it had greater initial accessibility, and because it was hoped that it would be the focal point of a larger area than Riverton itself.

There was no attempt in the initial or subsequent plans to establish a "green belt" or some other form of separation from the surrounding community. The land-ownership pattern did not lend itself to such treatment, since there are few if any economic incentives, and there was no desire on the part of the developers to create a separate enclave. Riverton Properties pointed out, however, that peripheral retail development, which takes advantage of the market created by Riverton residents, as well as nearby residential construction for families that could make use of the facilities provided within Riverton, could well create future difficulties if not controlled by the town.

Town Review of the PUD Application

The public hearing that was scheduled by the town board for May 20 and May 21, 1971, for consideration of the master plan describing planned unit development for Riverton presented the greatest public jeopardy for the project's future. Controversy had been minimal up to this point, but if a concerted public outcry emerged, then the town Board might consider conservative action and delay its approval.

An organized opposition to Riverton had been created in 1970 immediately after the passage of the town of Henrietta PUD ordinance. Citizens for Better Henrietta had organized themselves against the "Riverton Squeeze." The group, comprised of many residents aroused by Karz's earlier request for the Genesee Village zoning change, established a position of opposition to the Riverton proposal. Claiming that the ordinance was passed surreptitiously, the group wanted "to keep it like it is."

Literature distributed by the group during the winter of 1970 and spring of 1971 was filled with unfounded accusations and half truths (see Figure 5.2 and 5.3). Simon had assembled a staff and briefed them on the absolute necessity of avoiding controversy over the Riverton proposal.[25] His experiences at Reston with local government encouraged him to feel that a small vocal minority probably would not emerge into open community conflict (1) if uncommitted residents were convinced that the proposal was not detrimental to individual economic interests; and (2) if there was up to that time no antagonistic group directly engaged on any of the issues. At one public meeting Simon goaded the leaders of the opposition present into coming to grips with the problem, not of whether anything could be built, but of what to control and how. A team headed by Andrew Goldman, and made up of personable young staff members, prepared a strategy to support Simon's two points, should they become controversial issues. Goldman attracted several key staff members from the Rochester State UDC office whose local experience was to prove invaluable in denying "carpetbagger" references to

25. A search of the two Rochester newspapers and the local *Henrietta Post* for the critical two and one-half years of the proposal phase (1969–1972) showed the use of the word "controversy" only once. See *Henrietta Post*, Nov. 12, 1970.

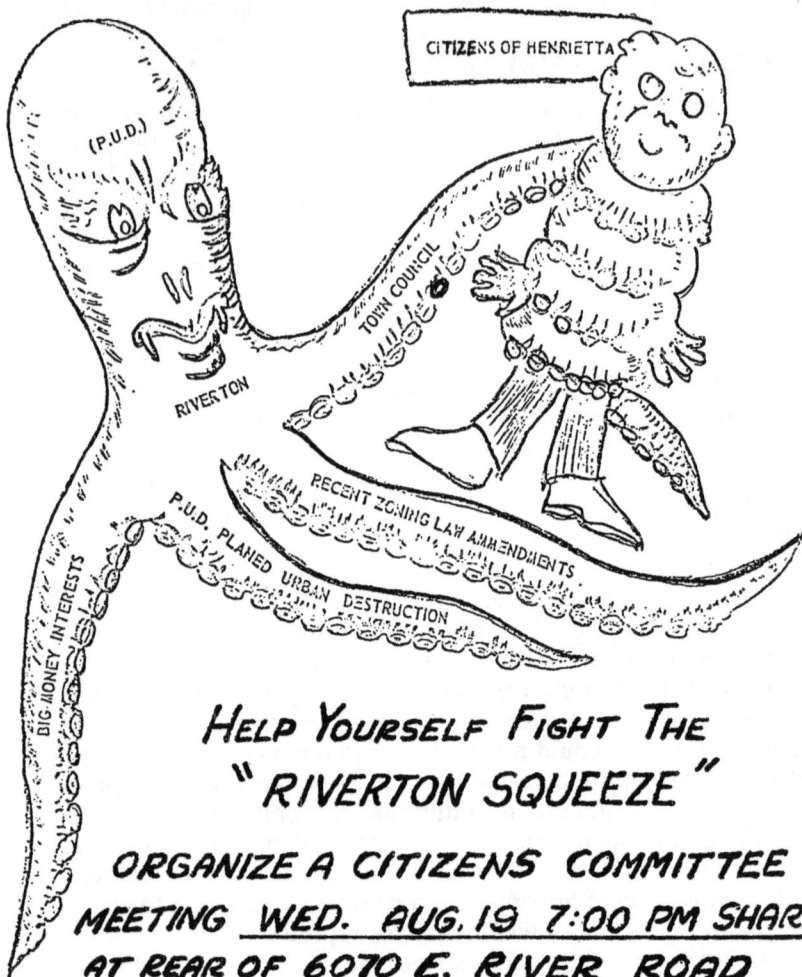

Figure 5.2. Flyer distributed in opposition to Riverton New Community

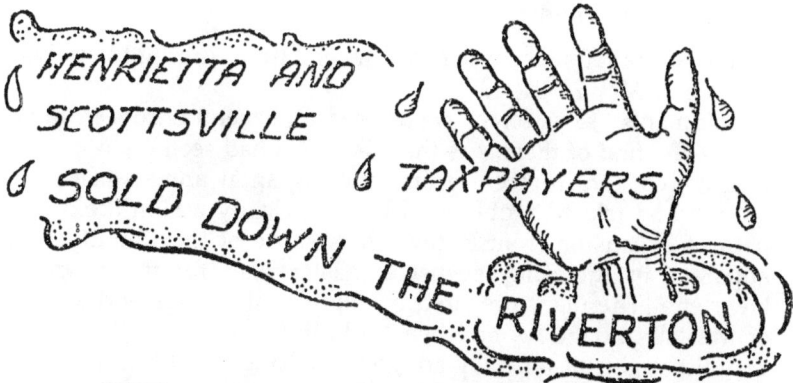

HENRIETTA AND SCOTTSVILLE TAXPAYERS SOLD DOWN THE RIVERTON

DO YOU KNOW THE HENRIETTA TOWN COUNCIL SOLD YOU THE TAXPAYERS " DOWN THE RIVERTON"?

DO YOU KNOW?

(1) When you were away on vacation your elected town council, over the objections of the citizenry, ammended the zoning laws so that anyone with 300 acres could build a town within a town without obeying the existing zoning laws.

(2) We in the area of Scottsville - Henrietta - Thruway area are to be sacrificed for the big money interests. We will get the direct traffic congestion, industrial pollution, property devaluation etc., etc., but all of Scottsville and Henrietta will have to pay the bill.

(3) All Scottsville and Henrietta will have to pay for schools (4), fire protection, and some form of law enforcement just to mention a few.

(4) The country look of this area will be gone forever. If we subsidize this one with our tax money and throw out all our zoning laws for every big money interest we will, in effect, bring the inner city and all its ills to the country.

If this project was a legitimate attempt for low priced housing they would not have to hire a public relation firm and a full time advance man to help slip this new tax burden into the Scottsville Henrietta area.

They would not have to use expensive productive farmland and attach like a leech to an over burdened, over taxed towns like Henrietta.

The Government engineers say the Mt. Morris Dam is no guarantee against flooding. Why this location?

This is an appeal to the silent majority of Henrietta and Scottsville. Are we going to be made fools of by self interest or are we going to brake the silence?

Remember the Riverton Corporation plans to cram 21,000 units with an average of 3 to 4 people a unit, combined with 300 to 400 acres of industry into our community.

If the project is so self-contained, why do we have to pick up the tab for the schools, etc.?

Your town council has eliminated the Planning Board, usurped its function, arbitrarily changed the zoning laws to facilitate Riverton, and all the future concentrations of overpopulation. This, of course, would not have been allowed under existing laws.

Although we have the right to vote down a Riverton school bond issue, according to the Town Council, we have no legal right to hold a referendum on Riverton which in one feld scoop would increase the population of Henrietta by 75 to 100 percent, not counting the industry.

Have the people of Henrietta lost the basic concept of a democracy? How can a Town Council that is suppose to represent the people perpetrate this tax burden on an already over burdened citizenry?

THINGS YOU CAN DO TO FIGHT RIVERTON.

Call a friend in Henrietta and Scottsville and tell it like it is. Riverton will not only disrupt and devaluate the area, it will hit us all in the pocketbook.

IT'S TIME TO RECLAIM OUR TOWN FROM THE POLITICIANS AND BIG MONEY DEVELOPERS.

Figure 5.3. Flyer distributed in opposition to Riverton New Community

Simon. (This reference was heard several times during the public hearing of May 20–21, 1971.)

Goldman's "sales force" capitalized on several factors in their favor. The first of these was that Henrietta had seen phenomenal land conversion in recent years, creating an awareness of urban growth and related problems. The town clearly was in the direct path of expansion from Rochester. A sense of inevitability was apparent in the comprehensive master plan for the town of Henrietta. The plan, prepared by the planning-engineering firm of Metcalf and Eddy, had been submitted in November, 1968, and although not officially adopted, had indicated that the portion of the township for which Riverton was proposed should permit planned unit development. The sales force also emphasized the importance of a "quality" project. (A sensitive approach to land development with innovations in human services was part of the Riverton prospectus.)

A form of instant credibility was created by identifying Robert Simon and Reston, Virginia, with the Riverton project. Presentations of the Riverton plans were accompanied by films and photographs of Reston to illustrate gracious living: lakes, open space, and bicycle paths free of automobile crossings. An alternative to urban sprawl did not have to be promised; the developer who did it once before not only could, but would, fulfill his promises.

Simon, Goldman, and other staff members in the days before the public hearing met with, in Simon's words, "anyone who would stand still long enough to listen." Any opposing voices were regarded as potential sources of incipient controversy. They were stilled by several endeavors. One was the "study committee" approach. A broad cross-section of residents of the town, and of the Rush-Henrietta School District were invited to become acquainted with the management staff and to present results of their meetings to the community. This proved to be a successful method of co-opting, as can be seen in the case of Riverton Fact-Finding Committee, Sub-Committee on Education; their undated mimeographed report concluded that "we are confident Riverton could be an asset as a well-planned community through the endeavors of Riverton Properties, Inc., the boards of the Town of Henrietta, and the Rush-Henrietta School Board."

The only formally organized group resisting the project prior to the town board hearing was the Citizens for Better Henrietta.

People organizing the group had been vocally opposed to the Henrietta PUD ordinance that passed in June, 1970. At this stage the developers treated them with respect and handled them cautiously. With behavior similar to that shown by the Homeowner's group at Lysander, their manner and style discouraged other members of the community who were disenchanted with the proposal from joining forces with them. Several members of the community who lived adjacent to the site and in other Stanndco developments were prominent in leading the opposition. Simon and Goldman dealt directly with them at several public meetings by treating them respectfully. The argument used to offset the effect of opposition was "not whether something will be built on the land, but what and how."

Recognizing that certain concerns existed in the community from the time of the Henrietta PUD ordinance hearing, Riverton management hired a research firm to conduct opinion polls of Henrietta residents. In summary, it appeared that project opposition relied upon one or more of the following misconceptions:(1) Riverton will lead to higher taxes for the area, by requiring new services without providing an adequate economic base; (2) Riverton will usurp existing governmental authority; (3) Riverton will overcrowd the schools; (4) Riverton will attract undesirable persons to Henrietta and bring problems heretofore thought to be indigenous to center cities; and (5) Xenophobia.[26]

Simon and his staff firmly believed that any opposition could be turned into support with an energetic program designed to inform the public of the true facts concerning Riverton. From the results of the opinion poll the developers concluded that "opposition . . . is based primarily on unreasoning fears, fears which can be overcome by informing the local population of Riverton's healthy economic base, people-oriented goals, design concepts and total development program. The experience at Reston had led the developer to believe that this opposition is capable of being overcome."

In preliminary presentations to the town and school boards, plans were generally accepted. Concern focused almost entirely

---

26. Confidential reports, submitted as Exhibits 39 and 40 in *Application for Guarantee Assistance* (Riverton Properties, Inc., Nov. 30, 1970). The reports, *Opinions and Knowledge of Henrietta Residents, Part I and Part II,* were prepared by the Harvey Research Organization (June–July, 1970).

on the fiscal impact: roads, utilities, schools, and other public services.

In Henrietta, approximately 70 percent of the local real estate taxes are used to support the public schools. Existing schools are overcrowded, and in recent years bond issues to build new ones have been rejected. A continuing effort was made by town and school officials to have Riverton pay as much of the community facility costs as possible. The school board wanted a donation of the first school.

Negotiations over who pays for what were long and tortuous. The school issue became a major stumbling block in achieving local approval. The school board wanted donation of the first school to be a condition of approval. Riverton maintained that it should be treated like any other developer, but then made a number of early concessions by agreeing to donate school sites and to build a connecting road.

The public hearing on the master plan for rezoning of the original 1,300-acre tract of Riverton land was held on May 20 and May 21, 1971. It was well attended and showed only scattered and inconsequential opposition: nearby property owners feared an increase in traffic congestion; others worried about the impact on taxes, or about the ability of the developers to carry through their plans. Interestingly enough, even though a broad range of housing was proposed, including housing for low-income families, no one objected to this aspect of the plan.

Comments of local residents indicated the success of the year-long public relations job done by the Riverton Properties staff. One of the most vocal and verbose critics of the project, one who regularly took hours of hearing time, commended the developers for: "a smooth and beautiful operation. We are overwhelmed." However, the statement of a co-chairman of the Riverton Fact-Finding Committee was the most eloquent testimony to the developers' efforts:

We worked with some intelligent people, we asked questions, we got answers. Consequently my thinking on Riverton has been changed a great deal. We can't stop growth in Henrietta. We have talked about planned development, we have asked for it, now it's being offered to us. This is the way to stop the kind of building we have had in the past in Henrietta. We have got apartment projects spinning up in our back yards. We appear at the Town Board or Zoning Board meetings and we oppose apartments. We can't tell them where we want them to put them but we know we don't want them in our backyards. So now, these people have come along and they offered us a possible solution, good planning. We can talk about our children, where will our children go in ten years from now? Where will they raise their families? We have to build, so why not with good planning. Riverton is a reality. Are we going to have good planned development or a repetition of the kind of development we have now? This land will be developed.[27]

The town adopted a zoning ordinance rezoning the 1,300 acres in July of 1971 but sidestepped the key issue of schools by stating that "prior to approval of the final site plan . . . the developer is required to make arrangements with the Rush-Henrietta School District to assure the availability of school facilities when needed." Settlement of the school issue was long in coming and was accomplished only through further concessions on the part of the Riverton developers. At one point in the discussion Simon informed the school board that for the developers to donate sites was not in the community's best interest. He said: "If the school board insists on our giving school sites, we'll give them. But, we think it's a poor idea. Riverton will have fewer community facilities."

Riverton Properties agreed to make up the difference in cash for the costs of educating children within Riverton over and above tax receipts for a period of two years and to match in cash 25 percent of any federal grants received by the town of Riverton for use in the construction of schools. The agreement further stipulated that Riverton Properties, whether it received grants or not, would pay the local share needed to retire the bonds for the first ten years (approximately 44 percent of the total) up to a maximum of $800,000. While the risk in reaching such an agreement was substantial, if the project were to proceed without lengthy delay there appeared to be no alternative. If federal grants for other supporting facilities were obtained later, they would lower the cost of development. There was no assurance, however, that grants would be forthcoming.

The Riverton developers also agreed to support any proposed legislation to levy a special assessment or "entrance fee" on each new household to help defray the capital costs of school construc-

27. *Rochester Times-Union*, March 19, 1971.

tion; and, subject to enabling legislation, they agreed to enter into lease or lease-purchase agreements with the school board.

Although concerned about the potential future costs of this agreement, the Riverton management felt it was the only way to reconcile the sensitive issue of schools. A hidden cost in these negotiations was the value of land to be set aside for new schools. Total land area of eighty-five acres for four elementary schools and a junior or senior high school could reach a value of $1 million. In the final analysis of the alternatives for dispelling potential conflict over schools, the developers felt that the agreement would help in increasing the chances for an early and successful vote on the required bond issue to construct the first school.

Regional and Federal Project Review

Having gained project approval from the town and school boards, the developers felt that public controversy had been successfully avoided. The proposal had only to move forward through the A-95 regional review and the final federal review for guarantee assistance. Both reviews were initiated simultaneously to expedite the starting of construction by spring, 1972.

Riverton's application to the Genesee-Finger Lakes Regional Planning Board, and one to the HUD New Communities Office for a loan guarantee for $12,000,000 were submitted in November, 1970. During the course of the review a number of serious problems were raised concerning specific aspects of the proposed development. Two fundamental questions were: (1) the proposed size of community, and (2) the proposed use of the flood plain for residential development. The full response to these and other questions required months of negotiations between various local, state, and federal agencies.

In order to overcome the two objections and maintain the character of the proposed new community, it was necessary to expand the project to include additional acreage adjacent to the site. Although no guidelines had been established, the HUD staff felt the project was too small. The revised plan included lands not yet under Riverton control, but which were later acquired. An additional 825 acres were added to the original development plan to reach a total of 2,560 acres. The additional acreage required substantial modification in the original site plan (see Tables 5.2

Table 5.2. Plans for Riverton land-use distribution

Type	Initial plan Acres	Percent of total	Revised plan Acres	Percent of total
Residential	860	56.9	1,046	44.8
Commercial	41	2.7	170	7.2
Industrial	327	21.7	400	17.1
Public and quasi-public	282	18.7	509	21.8
Land reserve	—	—	435	9.1
Total	1,510	100.0	2,560	100.0

Source: Final Environmental Statement, Riverton New Community, November 19, 1970, p. 93.

and 5.3). Although changes within the area under zoning review were minimized so as not to set back progress at the local level, the staff was in the awkward position of having to deal with two plans simultaneously.

Objections to building in the flood plain were met simply by eliminating plans for such development and by reorganizing much of the proposed open space. Expansion of the plan by purchase of additional land also allowed a more rational development to the east and further development of the internal road network. The New Communities Office was insistent in its requirement that Riverton make specific commitments to provide

Table 5.3. Riverton statistical information

	Initial plan	Revised plan
Population	21,120	25,600
Dwelling units	6,600	8,010
Single detached	2,300	2,800
Townhouses	1,250	1,520
Garden apartments	2,300	2,790
Medium high-rise	750	900
Gross residential density	4.3 dwelling units/acre	3.7 dwelling units/acre
Development period	13 years	16 years
Employment*	7,300	11,180

Source: Final Environmental Statement, Riverton New Community, November 19, 1970, p. 94.
*Number of jobs generated within the Riverton community.

low- and moderate-income housing during every stage of construction. HUD may have been particularly concerned about Riverton, as there was no low- or moderate-income housing built in Reston until after Simon was no longer actively involved in management decisions. Final agreement required the Riverton developers to provide 40 percent of all housing units for low- and moderate-income families with at least 10 percent for low-income families. The developers, in order to meet this target, further agreed to lower land prices for such units up to 15 percent below market price, and, to the extent grants were received, agreed that a portion of what was termed "cash flow benefits" (amounting to approximately 30 percent) were to be used for low- and moderate-income housing.

The A-95 review process moved forward (and sometimes sideways) during 1971. The revised plan submitted in February, 1971, was approved by the Regional Planning Board and was forwarded to HUD on September 28, 1971. Local support for the project was based on the proposal's presenting "a viable alternative to the continuation of suburban land development." Accompanying letters from private sources, including congressional representatives, endorsed the proposal. Congressman Horton in announcing the grant approval, as he did for Gananda, stated his strong support for the project. He felt the award was "particularly gratifying because my staff and I have spent many hours working to secure its approval." On December 22, 1971, Secretary George Romney of the United States Department of Housing and Urban Development announced a $12 million federal guarantee for the new community of Riverton, N.Y. The HUD final project agreement was completed on May 2, 1972.

Avoiding Controversy: A Continuing Task

Robert Simon had learned from his Reston, Virginia, experience that adoption of a new planned-unit development ordinance did not end his involvement with existing community residents and local governments. Depending on the ordinance content, a new-town developer can be subject to frequent local reviews, with each issue providing a potential source of community conflict.

Detailed site planning and provision of community services had moved forward during the A-95 and HUD project reviews.

The first-stage site plan was submitted for local review on a time-table dictated by HUD. Many revisions were necessary to meet objections by the town board before the first stage of 500 housing units and 50 acres of industrial and commercial development finally gained approval.

The program called for development of the first portion of the walkway system and a wide variety of housing types and designs. Community facilities included lighted tennis courts, an outdoor pool, the first community building, and playground areas. A major site-planning constraint was a zoning ordinance requirement to include 35 percent of the housing as single-family detached units in each stage of development. The developer was faced with a dilemma of satisfying local demands to avoid controversy, and meeting HUD requirements for low- and moderate-cost housing. This was resolved by taking the gamble of intermingling sale and rental housing throughout the site and reducing lot sizes. The average size of single-family lots was much smaller than normal for the suburbs around Rochester, and averaged 8,000 square feet. (The minimum lot size in Henrietta is 12,000 square feet and in some of the more affluent towns even higher.)

Not all of the controversy during preparation of the project site plan was imposed by outside agencies. Different methods of organizing the design phase of the proposal were tried.

Initially, all work was carried out by consultants, most of whom came from cities other than Rochester. A different-than-usual approach to site and architectural design was devised. Elsewhere, the typical approach is to select one firm to be responsible for this work, but at Riverton an overall master site planner and designer was engaged to locate all roads, walkways, building and parking areas, while individual "design architects" were to do preliminary plans for different townhouse, garden apartment, and patio-unit types and for prototype single-family homes. A single "control architect" was then to take all the preliminary building designs to working drawings. Simon believed the use of such an approach would avoid some of the problems he had faced in Reston. The control architect would provide the standardization and discipline necessary to keep costs down, and the site designer would give the overall continuity needed to prevent development of a series of "architected" clusters. Simon wanted a great variety of mix within any one complex of buildings along a given street.

Over a period of months, the approach required major adjustments. Architects of the caliber desired were not interested in doing only preliminary drawings to give "flavor" or "character," with no control over final drawings or construction. Long-distance review and coordination of the site plan proved virtually impossible. The system finally evolved to using fewer architects who carried their work through to the construction stage, with site-planning coordination and control performed by the Riverton staff.

In addition to gaining approval of the site plan, Riverton Properties pushed forward proposals for community services. Realizing that these were among the sensitive issues to local residents, the developers related conversations about facilities and services to Reston's achievements. Initial goals for community services were limited to those that Riverton Properties felt they could achieve through federal grants, and those that were absolutely necessary for successful marketing. Effective planning for these services is difficult for any private developer. If he tries to do too much, he is soon accused of paternalism and over-control. If he does nothing, he is accused of indifference and failing to meet his public responsibilities.

Columbia, Reston, and other large-scale building efforts have established some form of association as a basic vehicle for maintaining common property and carrying out various service activities. Local criticism of increased taxes to maintain Riverton facilities was overcome by the chartering of an internal form of common property management. Riverton intends to establish an Assocation, but with much broader representation than at Reston and with control turned over in a very short time to the residents.[28] The Association will be responsible for owning and maintaining common property, including the walkways, public open spaces, recreation facilities, and community buildings, and

28. The relationship between the Reston Association and the residents may not always be an harmonious one. Reston's citizens have had a number of confrontations with their Association and in 1967 a separate Community Association was set up by residents to give them a stronger voice in dealing with both the Reston Homeowners Association and the developer.

for the appointment of an architectural review board, as well as for enforcement of various controls on the use and maintenance of property.

To assist in getting community activities started, the first phase included a substantial commitment for facilities that will be owned and operated by the Association. This has sometimes been described as "pre-servicing" in contrast to the usual procedure of developing facilities only after there has been community pressure and there are resources available to do so. Strong advocates of participatory democracy might be concerned at the extent of facilities constructed before residents move in and have a chance to influence their design. However, both marketing strategy and the need to demonstrate that such facilities can build a sense of community make early construction essential.

The Riverton staff also committed much time and effort to other aspects of community development. Working with local institutions, applications were made to various governmental agencies and private foundations to initiate programs in the arts, comprehensive health services, an ecumenical religious program, and to establish an environmental studies center.

Summary

During the early phases of the project Robert Simon and his staff were optimistic about their chances to avoid community conflict and gain public acceptance of the proposal. They felt that local government in the Monroe County region was generally progressive. The area was described as a "bastion of Republicanism," the city and county both having Republican majorities on their respective legislative bodies. There is an increasing tendency for metropolitanization of the region's government, with more and more city functions being absorbed by the county. Such services as public mass transportation, public welfare, and public purchasing are performed by the county, with plans expected for other activities to follow suit. One of the factors that impressed Simon and first drew him into the project was referred to in the application to HUD for guarantee assistance:

Perhaps as important as formal government in the Monroe County region is the fact that public life is backed by a strong web of community-serving institutions headed by a large number of community-minded leaders. Such institutions as the Center for Governmental and Community Research, Fight, Metro-Act, the Universities, and the city and suburban newspapers see to it that a constant discussion of public issues at an admirably high level is maintained. Formal government is not left with the responsibility of identifying and defining major public issues.

The Riverton staff did a creditable sales job on the community residents, elected officials, and public employees. They had in their favor the transferred image of Reston to answer any questions about detail planning and site design. Quality of environment became a moot point because of the promise that what Simon had done before, he would do again.

In Simon's words, the reason for an avoidance of community conflict was that it became accepted that "Riverton is providing an intelligent plan for further growth in Henrietta, which will meet the needs of the area for more community facilities, while preserving permanent open spaces for varied outdoor pursuits." [29]

Unfortunately, the halcyon days anticipated by Simon were troubled. Town approvals to start construction consistently ran behind schedule, with the planning board taking the maximum time allowed under the ordinance before approving each phase. Applications, which had to be processed by the town offices prior to forwarding to Albany or Washington, had extraordinary delays. Preliminary site approval hoped for in April, 1972, did not come until June. Final approval was delayed long enough to postpone the start of construction until 1973. Events of this type led to the opinion stated by some that the relationship between the developers and the town had not always progressed smoothly.

The town fathers continued to worry about their image and expressed themselves in a resolution passed in August, 1972: "Riverton developers have consistently referred to the Riverton project as Riverton, New York, the new town of Riverton or other titles indicating a status independent of the Town of Henrietta." The resolution requested the developers to stop using such terms and to "indicate to the public that it is physically located within the Town of Henrietta and is proud to be a part of the dynamic

29. *HUD Challenge* (Washington, D.C., Aug., 1972).

program and development of the Town of Henrietta." The resolution passed unanimously.

Had events gone against Riverton Properties? Not necessarily. Simon, from his Reston experience, realized that the developer, in seeking a working arrangement with local government in the form of a PUD ordinance, subjects himself to possible controversy at every stage of project development. Not only must the elected officials and public employees be convinced at the presentation of an original master plan, they must remain convinced of the developer's capabilities.[30]

As in Gananda, an ongoing potential for conflict existed for Riverton Properties. The project history we have described covers a five-year period. Events during this period are used to summarize the Riverton project in regard to central issues of (1) the developer's leadership; (2) the nature or source of the proposal; and (3) the method of proposal presentation to the public.

Leadership of the Developer. There is clear evidence that Robert E. Simon was synonymous with Riverton in the minds of the residents of Henrietta. The local press gave prominence to Simon's involvement in Riverton, with constant references to his leadership at Reston. This identification carried over into the opinions of various public agencies in the region and the congressional representation. The esteem of those in the planning and development field for Reston, Virginia, gave Simon an ease of entrée to the Rochester area. Supporters for the project came forward because of the reputation Simon had established at Reston. Riverton Properties shifted identity from apartment-builder Karz to new-town-builder Simon.

Unlike Logue at Lysander, Simon was a frequent visitor to the community and made himself accessible to any forum available. Announcement of his presence at a public meeting usually promised a full-capacity audience. Simon remained in the forefront of project management through all of the possible exposures to controversy during the first four years of his involvement in the proj-

---

30. Simon's successors at Reston felt that this problem almost caused collapse of the project on several occasions. Commenting in *Professional Builder* (March, 1974), Chairman of the Board B. R. Dorsey said that Reston's success hinges on the attitude and actions of county and state governments with which the Reston developers must deal: ". . . conflicts with the county government have continued to concern the developer." See also Mahlon Apgar, IV, footnote 18, above.

ect. Only after construction had started and "pre-servicing" of the new community began did Simon shift from president of the company to chairman of the board.

From earlier descriptions there can be little doubt that Riverton was identified with Simon. However, this does not necessarily mean that Riverton Properties as an organization was identified with Simon. For example, Gananda's public relations suffered because of a lack of continuity between a strong personality leading the proposal and continuity of a staff to carry out the new-community plan. Public confidence in a project wanes with evidence of weak or unstable management. This was not the case in Riverton.

Because Simon was held in great respect in the planning and development field, he was able to attract competent, personable key people to Riverton Properties management. Andrew Goldman, executive vice president, joined the staff at the beginning of the assembling of the management. John Stainton, director of technical planning, and Scott Carlson, director of social programs, joined Goldman from the Rochester office of the New York State Urban Development Corporation. These key leaders shared Simon's views on development and were eager to participate in project management.

Simon personalized Riverton Properties by his style of leadership and firm belief in the role of the developer in building new communities. Simon's earlier role at Reston proved to be beneficial in gaining staff and local support for Riverton, even though his idealism and high design standards caused his eventual loss of control of Reston to the Gulf Oil Company. Idealism and principles are rare in developers, and Simon was respected by his staff and the community for these qualities.

Nature or Source of Proposal. What characteristics of the Riverton organization influenced public reaction to the developer? Conclusions derived from Riverton Properties' experience with elected officials and public employees indicate that a positive relationship resulted from the personalization of the organization. To rephrase this, Simon and staff represented a development concept with such sincerity and integrity that it was received by the community with a minimum of controversy. This positive aspect is beneficial in the early phases of local contact, but appears to have disadvantages over a longer period of time.

Whereas the public agency establishes a constant image by bureaucratic processes, the private corporation must continually reestablish and maintain its credibility. Doubts harbored by public-agency employees can prove detrimental to the prompt processing of applications for grants vital to success. Bitterness and jealousy harbored about a project's financial prospects can be seen as an antagonism to an individual more easily than to a public agency. Personal characteristics distasteful to a project opponent can justify a clerk's slow processing of a form more easily than if it were an impersonal agency he was dealing with.

Method of Proposal Presentation to Public. Riverton Properties' public relations strategy never deviated from the original two concepts: (1) Riverton had credibility because of Robert E. Simon and his identification with Reston, Virginia; and (2) Riverton represented the answer to "suburban sprawl" in the Rochester area.

Included in this strategy was the furtherance of an image of a "quality" project with substantial goals for incorporating community services at the developers' expense. Riverton Properties could select this path because of the evidence available from Reston. Compared to Lysander and Gananda, which could offer only promises, Riverton offered Reston as an illustration of ability to deliver. Support by the Riverton Fact-Finding Committee for the project is attributed to confidence in Simon and his management staff.

The strategy of complete disclosure of project plans, plus the developers' availability to meet with individual citizens, local government, or public agencies, was consistent throughout the critical early period of the project. Comments such as the following were published regularly in area newspapers: "There is a willingness on the part of the Riverton staff people to share all sorts of data with town leaders. If this could be continued, it would speak well for both the Town and the planned community."[31] This approach, of course, proved costly as concessions were made to overcome objections to specific project details. Simon and his staff felt that compromises resulted in a lasting negotiaton because of the elimination of future controversy on a specific issue.

31. Comment by Dr. Raymond Delaney, superintendent of the Rush-Henrietta School District, *Rochester Times-Union*, Feb. 17, 1971.

Robert Simon's words at a public presentation of the project summarize the impact of his leadership and influence on acceptance by the community: "For myself, I regard the planning and building of a new community as the most rewarding adventure of my life. It is an experience which stretches the mind and expands capabilities. I welcome others to the adventure."

Was Simon at Riverton more successful than Logue at Lysander or Moot at Gananda? The comparison of these projects and a review of the central issues set out in earlier chapters is discussed in the final chapter.

6 | Urban Development
and New Communities

The developer of one of America's most attractive and imaginative new communities regarded the planning and building of a new community as the most rewarding experience of his life: "The challenge . . . is heady wine, indeed."[1]

This sense of conviction is a strong personal commitment, a commitment which is difficult to find in other forms of urban development, for example, in school building, highway construction, urban redevelopment, and land subdivision. These do not, in comparison, stir the excitement, nor evoke the involvement of the entrepreneur. Thus, we have a dramatic type of development, supported by a deep involvement of the developer and brought before a community that probably has no previous experience to rely upon for coping with future events. The very term "new community," held with different meanings by different groups, creates portents of an overwhelming force. Self-interest and anxieties are raised to high levels when plans for development involving hundreds of millions of dollars, thousands of acres of land, and lengthy periods of building are first brought to a com-

1. Robert E. Simon, "The Challenge of Starting New Communities," in *HUD Challenge* (Washington, D.C., Aug., 1972). Simon was the developer of Reston, Virginia, and was recognized along with James Rouse, developer of Columbia, Maryland, as a pioneer in imaginative new-community development in the post–World War II era.

munity. The comprehensive nature of the new community, the requirement of resources, and the extended duration for the development process insure great public visibility.

The brief histories of Lysander (Radisson), Gananda, and Riverton followed the course of events for three development proposals for new communities. Although the characteristics of these three developments differ in scope and size, the sources of potential controversy are comparable. This final chapter summarizes the unique aspects of new-community development, reviews factors which affect development, and draws conclusions from the analyses of the three communities studied.

As a subject of theoretical investigation and practical application, the new-community concept has aroused international interest: as a speculative venture, a method of achieving idealistic social and economic goals, and as an element of national policy.[2] Ebenezer Howard's slim volume, *Garden Cities of To-Morrow*,[3] first published in 1898, set forth principles for urban development that provide a response to the effects of industrialization and urbanization upon the individual, the family, and society. Eighteenth- and nineteenth-century utopian thinkers grappled with these problems, evolving theories that saw application in northern Europe and North America. The dominant intellectual tradition supporting these theories was antiurban: praising nature and warning against the dangers of urban life. It was against this background that the new-town movement gained support in the 1930's. However, the war diverted the nation's interest during the 1940's, and the postwar period was one of unparalleled suburban growth. By the 1950's, the continuing movement to the suburbs had forced a re-evaluation of suburban living; a change

2. Comparative data on the characteristics of ten federally assisted new communities is found in Hugh Mields, Jr., *Federally Assisted New Communities* (Washington, D.C.: Urban Land Institute, 1973). A typical project such as Jonathan, Minnesota, is expected to reach a population of 50,000 in 20 years; it requires the purchase of 8,194 acres and over $150,000,000 in capital for the project's first ten years. A positive annual cash flow is projected for the ninth or tenth year—the first profitable year for sixteen years after development started.

3. Ebenezer Howard, *Garden Cities of To-Morrow* (Cambridge, Mass.: The M.I.T. Press, 1965). First published as *To-Morrow: A Peaceful Path to Reform* (1898).

of climate evolved in which a suburban alternative to sprawl was welcome.

What has been called the "urban-development critique"[4] has led to the discouraging conclusion that, in the growth of urban America, pressures of necessity and expediency have ruled, producing a series of uninspired cities and towns put together in response to immediate needs, with all too little attention paid to ultimate goals and a satisfying environment. One reaction to these problems has been the attempt to achieve planned, orderly urbanization patterns through the development of "new towns" and "new communities."

A national commitment to solve the problems of urbanization and to provide orderly urban development was expressed in the Housing and Urban Development Acts of 1968 and 1970: These two programs—(1) New Communities Program: Loan Guarantees and Supplementary Grants (Title IV of the 1968 Act); and (2) New Communities Assistance Program (Title VII of the 1970 Act)—have resulted in thirteen new towns being launched between 1970 and the end of 1972 (fifteen by the end of 1973). Clearly, not everything that is called a "new town" is a new town. The prototype of the concept of "new towns" in their purest form is found in Europe, particularly in the United Kingdom.[5] Our use of the British term is significant, because we have been influenced by their experience and because their goals, policies, and practice provide norms with which other more limited approaches can be compared.

It is well to keep in mind the general objectives sought in the design and execution of new towns in Europe. The new-town program was undertaken initially to relieve population pressures in intensively built-up metropolitan areas by reducing the concentration of population and places of employment, while allowing rebuilding of existing central cities. Another objective was to provide a pattern for urbanization that would produce employ-

4. Edward P. Eichler and Marshall Kaplan, *The Community Builders* (Berkeley, Calif.: University of California Press, 1967), pp. 1–10.

5. An overview of the new towns in Great Britain can be found in Sir Frederick J. Osborn and Arnold Whittick, *The New Towns: Answer to Megalopolis* (London: McGraw-Hill, 1963) p. 7. See also Peter Self, *New Towns: The British Experience* (New York: John W. Ley, 1972).

ment opportunities in depressed and underdeveloped rural and agricultural areas that were losing population to the large cities.

Planned and deliberate attempts to develop new open communities that offer a full complement of commercial and industrial activities and both economic and social integration are a fairly recent phenomenon in the United States.[6] Variations of such planned developments date back to 1663 when Dutch Mennonites established the first communal colony in America in what is now Lewes, Delaware. By 1858, some 130 different utopian settlements had begun in the United States in locations ranging from Oneida, New York; Ephrata, Pennsylvania; to Nauvoo, Illinois; and New Harmony, Indiana. The "utopian" aspects of new-town development deserve attention here, if only briefly, because for the most part developers who are involved in the new-town programs in the United States have demonstrated a genuine and sincere desire to make things better, and this particular goal has provided the primary impetus to their involvement in the program. Their commitment is as much to "build a new city" as it is to make a profit.

The new communities being built in the United States today are characterized by their scale of development, the management arrangements for their development, and their comprehensive and inclusive original plan. The definition of new community used in the Advisory Commission on Intergovernmental Relations report will be useful here.

New communities are large-scale developments constructed under single or unified management, following a fairly precise, inclusive plan and including different types of housing, commercial and cultural facilities, and amenities sufficient to serve the residents of the community. They may provide land for industry, offer other types of employment opportunities, and may eventually achieve a considerable measure of self-sufficiency. With few exceptions, new communities under development today are within commuting distance of existing employment centers.[7]

6. For a more detailed discussion of the history of American new towns, and federal involvement in such efforts, see Advisory Commission on Intergovernmental Relations (ACIR), *Urban and Rural America: Policies for Future Growth* (Washington, D.C., April, 1968). Also, the origins of modern new towns are described by a pioneer in the field: Clarence Stein, *Toward New Towns for America* (New York: Reinhold, 1957).

7. ACIR, *Urban and Rural America*, pp. 63–64.

Of particular significance is the idea of an initial plan incorporating the ultimate geographic area of the community and providing for a predetermined population size. If the only difference between suburban subdivisions and new communities were superlatives of size, then we could attribute distinctive characteristics to scale. A truer picture can be formed from the *process* of development and the *objectives* of the development program.

The development process for a new community provides marked contrast to the typical suburban land-development approach in three different aspects. First, in new-community development, the private sector is organized and coordinated by one management unit. There is a centralized decision-making process, a core unit responsible for the planning and executing of not only the overall project but also the individual parts of the development. Second, the entire area encompassed by the new community is developed in accordance with a plan and a schedule which describe not only what is to be done, but also when and by whom. This planning and scheduling is necessary before the new-community developer is able to secure commitments from private lenders and public agencies. Third, the existence of a centralized decision-making unit within the new-community developer's organizational structure offers all those agencies within the public sphere a single focal point with which to deal.

The objectives of the development program must exceed the basic profit motive because of the low rate of return on capital.[8] In what Robert E. Simon describes as "the challenge of starting new communities," we find that the *development objectives* become translated into development opportunities.

Among the wide range of purposes which have motivated those who have embarked on the hazardous project of new-community planning and construction, one common characteristic of such undertakings has been the development of large tracts

8. Discussion of the economics of developing new communities can be found in Robert D. Wilburn and Robert M. Gladstone, *Optimizing Development Profits in Large Scale Real Estate Projects* (Washington, D.C.: Urban Land Institute, 1972). See also: Mields, *Federally Assisted New Communities*, pp. 139–146. Mields sums up the developer's risks as (1) extremely large carrying costs over a long period of time; (2) uncertainty with regard to changes in the external economy and governmental relations; (3) heavy overhead and start-up costs; (4) management of land development, community facilities, and citizen participation; (5) economic failures that do not become apparent until the last several years of development.

under one ownership and the provision of a fairly precise, inclusive plan for all of the ultimate geographic area that incorporates some of the facilities and amenities for the whole community—which normally would not be available until a considerably later period. Within the framework of a well-planned environment responsive to social and economic needs and goals, there has usually been a desire to provide quality housing, public facilities and services, and amenities unavailable in conventional tract subdivisions. Although it has been recognized that certain of these objectives could be achieved through the extensive planning and supervision of any large-scale urban development, it has been contended by some that the building of new communities offers greater opportunities for the realization of the full potential of large-scale urban development.

Ebenezer Howard saw the opportunities (in the light of reformism) as a solution to the ills of urban nineteenth-century England by providing the advantages of "town" and "country" in a single Garden City (see Figure 6.1).

The advantages in new-community development, first enunciated by Howard, were reiterated over seventy years later in the Housing Acts of 1968 and 1970. As the problems resulting from urbanization of the nation's expanding population became more serious, the planning and construction of new communities are viewed as unparalleled opportunities to combine private enterprise and business objectives with the broader social, economic, and political goals of American society. The achievement of such goals depends largely on the nature of the development group and the extent of governmental participation.

Factors Affecting the Development Process

New-town planning for the independent private developer is a complex task which must incorporate the subterfuges of land assembly with the persistence necessary for the years of implementation. Rouse's dealings in the 1950's and early 1960's with the Howard County Board of Commissioners (at Columbia) typify the task of the private developers in gaining public acceptance of development projects.

A point to be made, however, is that after the federal legislation of 1968 and 1970, *all* future urban development will be in-

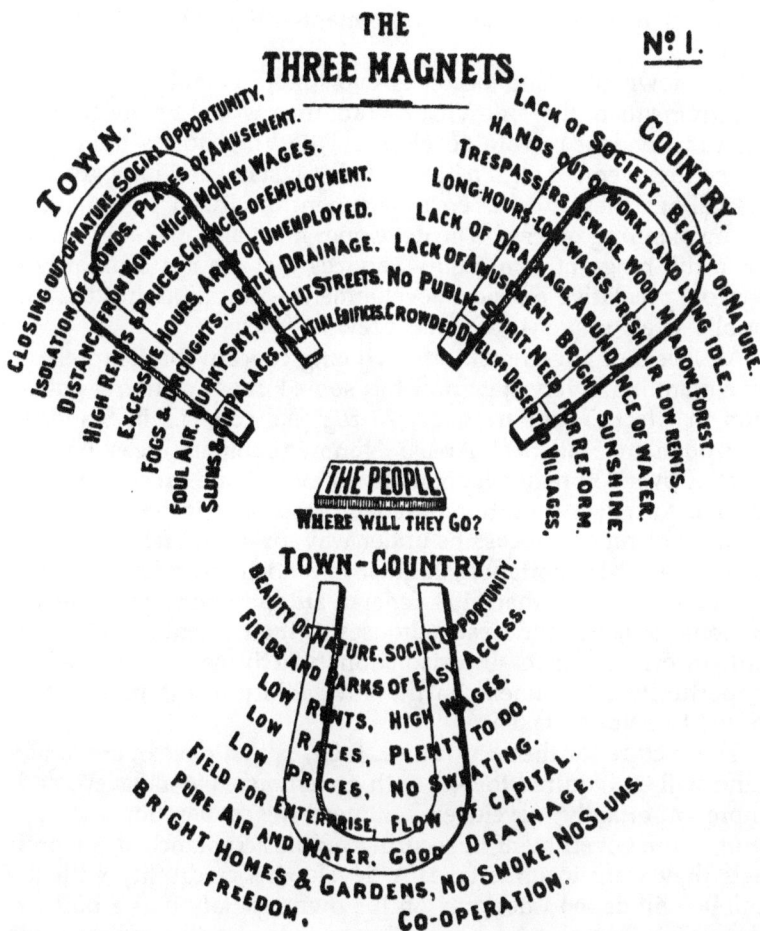

Figure 6.1. Ebenezer Howard's "Three Magnets" (1898) illustrates the advantages of living in a "garden city." Reprinted from Ebenezer Howard, *Garden Cities of To-Morrow*, by permission of The M.I.T. Press, Cambridge, Massachusetts. Copyright 1965 by The M.I.T. Press.

creasingly subject to government intervention, particularly as concern for protection of the physical environment becomes more acute, and as local governments—especially small jurisdictions—become more conscious of the increasing costs that conventional new residential development brings to local government.[9]

New-town planning becomes even more complex under the requirements of the Title VII program than would be the case for the independent private developer. Title VII requires the developer's involvement with a host of federal, state, and local governmental agencies and his encouragement of citizen participation in the planning process. The developer must also make provision for a full range of community services that are not ordinarily a part of speculative physical development—education, health, and public safety systems, to name a few.

All levels of government are evincing concern for comprehensive planning. Every state now has some kind of planning operation in effect. There are over 270 regional councils in Standard Metropolitan Statistical Areas. Nonmetropolitan areas have a total of over 330 regional councils, in every state except a few of the most rural. A condition of federal assistance is that a comprehensive planning process be under way for water and sewer systems, mass transportation, highways, and housing supply. Applicants for more than 100 federal aid programs must notify regional or statewide clearinghouses of their intention to file for aid, in order to give all jurisdictions which may be affected an opportunity to comment on the advisability of the project proposed to be undertaken.

The picture for the near future, then, is that developers of any kind will be required to deal with governments at all levels, and, more importantly, developers will need the cooperation and support of the government in securing public acceptance of the projects they want to undertake. A developer's credibility with the public will depend not only on his own reputation as a builder-developer, but also on his ability to convince the governments involved of the adequacy of his planning, and of his ability to deliver the product he has promised without undue adverse impact on the environment or local tax structure.

Unlike the building of small, individual development projects, the new-community developer must work closely with local government agencies to secure a variety of public services and to as-

9. The cognizance of local governments for the need to control development has been well described by Fred Bosselman and David Callies, *The Quiet Revolution in Land Use Controls* (Washington, D.C., 1971).

sure compliance with legislated requirements. Furthermore, because of its greater size and complexity, the new-community developer's relationships with local governmental agencies extend over a much longer period of time. Since most proposed new-community sites are in rural areas with existing local governmental jurisdictions, it becomes important to identify which units of government make decisions affecting the development site. The importance of local government structures in cases of community conflict touches on the questions of where the developer must go within the structure to get governmental rulings and decisions to execute his development plan. Governmental structures are likely to be informal and not clearly defined in rural areas. Thus the developer is required to know which agency handles which problems if he is to avoid controversy over his proposal.

The involvement of local, state, and federal levels of government in regulating elements of urban development is summarized in Table 6.1.

Land-use Controls. A major event in the urban-development process is the local review of a planning project for conformance with land-use controls. Land-development concepts as comprehensive as those needed for a new community are unlikely to have been considered in a municipality's existing zoning ordinance, subdivision, regulations, or official map. While conventional land-use regulations are still adequate for regulating developments in most built-up communities, they are totally inadequate and often misused in guiding development in rapidly urbanizing areas.[10]

The incompatibility of a development proposal with existing ordinances requires legislative action to modify or amend existing statutes, or to create new acts where none appropriately treat the proposal. Most jurisdictions have an advisory body and, in some cases, a technical staff, to assist in reviewing requests for legislation relating to land-use controls. The public hearings and

---

10. ACIR, *Urban and Rural America*, p. 121. The influence of land-use controls on urban land development is treated at length by the National Commission on Urban Problems (Douglas Commission), *Research Report no. 11* (Washington, D.C., 1968) and with reference to new communities in the ACIR study. Both studies describe the frustrations of trying to succeed at the local level with projects of a complexity beyond the capacity for evaluation by elected governing bodies.

Table 6.1. Role of government at local, state, and federal levels in regulating urban facilities

Elements of urban development	Counties PLN	ACQ	FIN	CON	OPR	REG	Municipalities PLN	ACQ	FIN	CON	OPR	REG
Transportation												
Expressways and freeways												
Tollways												
Major highways												
Collector highways	X	X	X	X	X							
Secondary roads	X	X	X	X	X		X	X	X	X	X	
Bridges and viaducts	X	X	X	X	X		X	X	X	X	X	
Urban streets							X	X	X	X	X	
Airports		X										
Public transportation (bus and rail lines)												
Parking facilities							X	X	X	X	X	
Street lighting							X			X	X	X
Utilities												
Water supply	X	X	X	X	X	X	X		X	X	X	
Sanitary sewers	X	X	X	X	X	X	X	X	X	X	X	X
Sewerage treatment plants	X	X	X	X	X	X	X	X	X	X	X	X
Storm drainage and flood control	X	X	X	X	X	X	X	X	X	X	X	X
Electricity, gas and telephone service												
Refuse removal and disposal	X	X	X	X	X	X	X	X	X	X	X	X
Health												
Clinics and medical services					X	X					X	X
Hospitals and paramedical facilities	X	X	X	X	X	X						
TB sanitariums	X	X	X	X	X							
Public safety												
Police protection				X						X		
Correctional facilities	X	X	X	X	X							
Fire protection										X		
Recreational facilities												
Parks							X	X	X	X	X	
Playgrounds							X	X	X	X	X	
Forest preserves	X	X	X									
Indoor recreational and meeting facilities							X	X	X	X	X	
Libraries							X	X	X	X	X	
Education												
Primary and secondary schools				X								
Trade and vocational schools				X								
Adult education facilities				X								
Junior colleges												
Colleges and universities												
Housing and redevelopment							X	X	X	X	X	
Civic, governmental and municipal buildings and facilities	X	X	X	X	X	X	X	X	X	X	X	X

Source: Advisory Commission on Intergovernmental Relations, *Urban and Rural America: Policies for Future Growth* (Washington, D.C., 1968).
Key: PLN = Planning; ACQ = Acquisition of sites and coordination; FIN =

Special districts and school districts						State government						Federal government		Remarks
PLN	ACQ	FIN	CON	OPR	REG	PLN	ACQ	FIN	CON	OPR	REG	FIN	REG	
						X	X	X	X	X		X		
						X	X	X	X	X		X		
						X								
X	X	X	X	X								X	X	Public transportation is operated privately.
X		X	X	X										
X	X	X	X	X										Privately owned utilities provide a large proportion of water supply, electricity, gas, telephone and refuse disposal services.
X	X	X	X	X				X						
								X	X				X	
								X	X				X	
							X							Hospital and paramedical facilities are primarily provided through private means.
X	X	X	X	X								X	X	
							X							
X	X	X	X	X										
X	X	X	X	X										
X	X	X	X	X										
X	X	X	X	X										
X	X	X	X	X					X	X				
X	X	X	X	X					X	X		X		
X	X	X	X	X			X		X	X				
X	X	X	X	X					X	X				
				X	X								X	

Financing; CON = Construction; OPR = Operating; REG = Regulatory and/or policy making.

notification of local residents offer the opportunity for constitution of an opposing body; thus, the full-fledged zoning controversy is created.

Studies of zoning controversies enable us to identify the motives of the local executive body as (1) protection and improvement of the community; (2) minimizing of tax increases; and (3) resolution of community issues in a manner satisfying the greatest number of residents.

The zoning issue, in effect, becomes a critical point, if not the most important one, in the success of a development proposal. Conclusions about public participation in land-development decisions for zoning are similar to those centered on urban renewal. Community participation, and in most cases the concomitant controversy, are related to pecuniary and personal considerations. Generally, the primary reason for interest by property owners other than those in the immediate vicinity are related to the possible precedent which may more directly affect them in the future.[11]

Issues involving zoning and subdivision controls are characterized by: (1) the fact that decisions are made on the *local* level; (2) the *individualized* character of decisions; and (3) the *community participation* which may be generated if the decision becomes controversial. Various observers of suburban politics have recounted issues which generated into full-fledged zoning controversies: Robert C. Wood described the politics of suburbia and the values inherent in the policies of suburban units of government;[12] Murray S. Stedman described the problems of housing and land as being in the forefront of suburban political controversy because these considerations go to the very heart of suburban living.[13] The bitterness of debate in zoning controversies is based on the potential jeopardy of a major family investment. Whatever action is or is not taken, the impact on an individual family is highly personal.

11. James Q. Wilson, *Urban Renewal* (Cambridge, Mass.: The M.I.T. Press, 1966), p. 407.

12. The multiplicity of governmental units has been commented on at length in publications of the Advisory Commission on Intergovernmental Relations. See also Robert C. Wood, *Suburbia: Its People and Their Politics* (Boston: Houghton Mifflin, 1958).

13. Murray S. Stedman, *Urban Politics* (Cambridge, Mass.: Winthrop, 1972), p. 56.

The advantages of local government's involvement in land-development decision-making are similar to traditional arguments in favor of home rule: those who reside in a community know best how to determine its future. This in turn bolsters support for local government by residents. Even though today the state and federal governments are increasingly assuming responsibility for many decisions formerly made by local government, the basic development decisions regarding residential, commercial, and industrial development in municipalities are still made by the local government.

The disadvantage of localized land-development decision-making is that such decisions are frequently made on the basis of narrow considerations limited to the local level. The nature of new communities reflects comprehensive regional and, possibly, national issues. Although broad policy issues do have an impact on local residents, overall effects exceed those interests typically identified at the local level. Literature on zoning controversies amply illustrates the subtle and complex issues and interests which figure in land-development decisions, and perhaps indicates why the right decision is not easy to ascertain. The question is, frequently: right for whom? What may be in the general public interest of the local community may not be in the interest of the larger metropolitan community. Harder yet is the problem of minority interests versus the interests of the majority. Otherwise, it is a matter of counting or estimating votes on each side of the issue, clearly not very satisfactory for the community issue.

The interests of local governing bodies tend to be of a conservative nature. Generally, these bodies want to preserve the community in its existing physical form, and perhaps extend and consolidate that form; retain the same type of citizenry, and generally avoid radical changes and risk-taking. Most suburban communities are primarily residential, and it is the residents, in their role as residents and tax-payers, who elect local governments—thus fostering the conservative nature of local governments.

A major positive concern of local governing bodies is to improve the tax base so as to offer basic governmental services, or improve services, without raising property taxes. Almost all municipalities tend to be dissatisfied with their tax position, and many are truly caught in a tax squeeze—especially in rapidly growing areas which must build from scratch the basic urban capital plant, relying almost entirely on the local property tax revenues.

Public hearings on land-use controls are the forum for community participation, permitting a broad base for local involvement. The extent to which zoning and subdivision decision-making impinge on public awareness may be partially measured by reading local newspapers, where such matters figure prominently. The primary advantage of community participation in land-development issues is the sustenance of a continuing dialogue between residents and local officials, thus assuring a responsiveness to public opinion. In addition, community participation may have important ramifications beyond the actual land-development issue at hand.

Disadvantages of community participation stem from the negative aspects of participation, or from the lack of involvement. Controversy over land-development issues can have divisive effects of a virtually permanent nature on a community. James Coleman cited the influence of previous controversy on new issues and the detrimental effect on community relations.

Public apathy toward zoning decisions draws little public notice. Moreover, public interest is sometimes dampened by the attitude, often firmly based, that the planning board, board of appeals, or village board will listen politely at the public hearing and then do as it pleases unless besieged by a mob of irate citizens. More importantly, it is a fact of political behavior that apathy or silence implies consent, while activity is usually motivated by opposition. Most people who come to public hearings want to raise their voices in opposition to the proposal under discussion. This does not make public hearings a waste of time; but public hearings—and subsequent newspaper coverage of them—tend to emphasize opposition to any given project. This is likely to prove fatal to unusual projects, such as new-community proposals. Mediocre development proposals, arousing little response of any kind, are more likely to be approved.

A typical land subdivider or commercial developer works on a scale that limits his public-agency contacts to the local level of government. He finds that personal contact with elected officials or public employees eases working relationships. However, the comprehensive nature and size of a proposed new community makes inevitable an involvement with levels of government above the local level. For those new-community developers seeking federal assistance of any form this involvement is a certainty, usually with regional or area-wide planning agencies with jurisdiction over a multiple number of governments.

Major pieces of federal legislation have placed the responsibility for area-wide planning with the appropriate regional body, and the influence of the federally imposed system on land-development proposals is significant for new communities. In addition to the impact of land-use controls as interpreted by the local governing body, a regional clearinghouse must receive assurances that a proposal is locally accepted. In effect, the requirements for gaining governmental subsidies for new communities mandate a full hearing of local sentiments by the clearinghouse. Adverse criticism evolving out of a controversial planning proposal can result in disapproval by a regional body. Looked upon separately from a regional planning agency which has only advisory powers, the clearinghouse review body can be as effective as a regional or county legislative agency in preventing the development of a new community.

In the three upstate New York communities discussed above, developers were affected by issues beyond the local level and, in turn, were forced to deal with influences from the county, regional, state, and federal governments. For example, the requirements of the Environmental Protection Agency were more demanding in terms of development costs than those of any other levels of government. It is axiomatic that as a development becomes more complex in scope, that is, with respect to the area under development, the magnitude of costs, the varied services being delivered, and the time period for completion, the more susceptible a project becomes to the larger national criteria and processes.

The three studies show that local communities do not exist in isolation from statewide and federal levels of control. Federal agencies have mandated that the states provide area-wide planning by an appropriate regional body as a requisite for assistance from a wide range of federal programs. But beyond this is the mandatory compliance with environmental responsibilities for the commitment of any funds to a local government for a particular project. Thus, by federal mandate a community must require a developer to provide a commitment of adherence to standards that may be contrary to the requirements of local public investment, regulatory ordinances, and economic-incentive devices. Recent federal legislation has passed the burden of preparing such commitments, in the form of Environmental Impact Statements to local government, which has passed this along to the developer.

In addition to government influences on development, the local power structure also affects the development process. Understanding and analyzing the local power structure can be of critical importance in determining where and how community conflict may evolve. What the developer is concerned with in new-community proposals is: Who are the individuals who have the power to get things done?

Developers operate intuitively by seeking out "community leaders," as well as elected officials, in their efforts to gain acceptance for development proposals. The implications for new-community development are that the developer will need cooperation from government officials for a successful project. In less-developed parts of the country, where governmental institutions are not sophisticated and much local governmental business is handled on a somewhat informal basis by the "town fathers," knowledge, or the lack of knowledge, of who are the effective decision-makers can make or break a proposal for land development.

There is an extensive body of literature in political science and sociology with reference to identification of the important personages in political decision-making.[14] A proposed new-community development would constitute such a major social issue. Political scientist Robert Dahl, in *Who Governs?*[15] is representative of one school of thought in suggesting that important political decisions are influenced in the main by a pluralist body of political decision-makers, with the *particular* decision-makers changing from issue to issue in the community. Sociologist Floyd

14. For a bibliography on the subject, see Charles M. Bonjean, Terry N. Clark, and Robert L. Lineberry, *Community Politics: A Behavioral Approach* (New York: The Free Press, 1971), pp. 372–387.

15. Robert A. Dahl, *Who Governs?* (New Haven: Yale University Press, 1965).

Hunter in *Community Power Structure* [16] suggests, on the other hand, that all major public issues are determined by a very small number of community influentials or power holders.

In any event, these authors and others are in agreement as to the importance of identifying the community power structure in order to affect community decision-making. Furthermore, these two schools of thought agree that persons who really influence community decisions often may not be members of the legalistic or institutional governmental structure. Since these political power brokers may be crucial in determining local government and other institutional cooperation or hostility to the developer's proposals, the matter of identifying the local power structure becomes an important aspect of the developer's ability to minimize controversy and, as a consequence, to secure success.

Summary

In 1972, ten years after he started land acquisition for Columbia, Maryland, James Rouse ruminated on the reasons for the existing community's acceptance of the project proposal. He observed that "people give us credit for doing a whale of a selling job. We really didn't. We dealt with the county responsibly. We answered every call. The simple fact of promising to do suburban development well instead of badly is what sold us. People came to believe that we had integrity about what we were doing." [17] Rouse's formula for gaining acceptance and avoiding community conflict over a comprehensive development scheme oversimplifies the complex issues involved in the process. In our three illustrations, these issues are part of a complex phenomenon.

Earlier, we put forward three key factors to assist in understanding the emergence of controversy over land development: (1) the characteristics of the parties involved in a controversy; (2) the specified set of relations between them; and (3) the parties' environment or context. These factors suggested central issues concerned with the developer's leadership, the effects of the developer's organization on public reaction, and the influence of

16. Floyd Hunter, *Community Power Structure* (Chapel Hill: University of North Carolina Press, 1953).

17. Gurney Breckenfeld, *Columbia and the New Cities* (New York: Ives Washburn, 1971), p. 272.

the methods of proposal presentation on the emergence of controversy.

Observing events during the proposal phase of three new communities provides the opportunity to review the importance of the central issues we have selected and to add other important issues that have come to the surface. This chapter summarizes these observations and suggests future research leading toward a greater understanding of community conflict over urban land development.

The theoretical background for this book was derived from general studies on social conflict, and, specifically, from James Coleman, Louis Kriesberg, Raymond Mack, and Richard Snyder. It is important to recall that these authors looked at controversy as a dynamic process of relationships between parties and between parties and their environment.

In each of the three new-community proposals we found that the parties representing the proposal were clearly identified for the community at the beginning of the project. For example, Lysander neighbors knew that a state agency, the recently formed Urban Development Corporation, headed by Edward Logue, was purchasing land and evaluating the site for development. Wayne County neighbors of Gananda were introduced to Stewart Moot and his first partners by public information releases as land was being acquired. Similarly, when Milton Karz was rebuffed in Henrietta, Robert Simon immediately came forward in the organization to create a new image for Riverton. Thus, in each case we have the identification of individuals acting as leaders or as leaders of organizations as parties in the interactional relationship.

The other side of the relationship, that is, between parties, is less precisely described.[18] The opposition role is usually performed by the elected leadership of the community acting as the community elite. Whereas most of the literature on the subject operates on the assumption that conflict is articulated and resolved at critical points in the development process by two parties, our examples show otherwise. This assumption was not

18. Kriesberg recognizes that "conflict units do not stand alone. There are possible allies, expanded constituencies and more encompassing organizations and groups." See Louis A. Kriesberg, *Sociology of Social Conflict* (Englewood Cliffs, N.J.: Prentice-Hall, 1973), pp. 137–39.

supported by events in the three existing communities. In Ly-sander and Henrietta, in addition to elected officials, citizens committees were formed to represent the interests of a third party in the relationship. While we tend to look at participants in the process as parties, that is, as individuals representing exist-ent groups, there are effective activities by individuals acting out of self-interest which lead to organized opposition or sup-port. In all three illustrations individual actions did lead to the formation of another party in the conflict relationship.

The third factor we have used to aid in understanding emergence of controversy is the environmental context of a con-flict. Attitudes, behaviors, and goals of parties to the conflict are shaped by the context in which they exist. An important factor in predisposing a community to any kind of precipitating event lies in what Coleman described as the "residuum of controversy."[19] For example, the degree and intensity of previous controversy in-fluenced the continued conflict in Henrietta. Early disputes with Karz and other developers sustained activities against Riverton after major public confrontations had been resolved favorably for the developer. The acrimony of the debate at the initiation phase of the proposal at Lysander was sustained during the later stages of the project. These attitudes supported a drive to limit UDC powers on a statewide basis. The lack of previous controversy over land development in western Wayne County aided the de-veloper in minimizing controversy during the course of the Ga-nanda project. Moot and his successors were able to deal with the issues at hand and not with hidden agendas of unstated griev-ances.

In terms of the "residuum of controversy" we find that conflict at Riverton was influenced by previous development in Henrietta. Although the Baldwinsville area had some controversy before the Lysander proposal, the strength of early debates car-ried on to later relations between UDC and the community. At Gananda, the lack of previous development controversy left the developer free from this obstacle. A summary of the community

19. The observation was that "a difference which leads some communities to respond to an incident with conflict and allows others to pass it by is the past his-tory of controversy in the community, which may have created mutual antago-nisms or fostered unity." See James S. Coleman, *Community Conflict* (New York: The Free Press, 1957), p. 7.

Table 6.2. Areas of community concern toward development proposals
in Lysander, Gananda, and Riverton

Lysander:
1. Effect on present way of life
2. Economic impact on the individual or household
3. Prospect of minority groups being brought into area as residents of new
   community[a]

Gananda:
1. Effect on taxes
2. Structure and relation of existing governmental bodies to Gananda
3. Possibility of overloading existing community services, including, but not
   limited to, schools
4. Economic impact on the area
5. Impact of large population growth on the area[b]

Riverton:
1. Effect on taxes by requiring new services without providing an adequate
   economic base
2. Usurpation of existing governmental authority
3. Overcrowding of schools
4. Possibility of attracting undesirable persons indigenous to center cities
5. Xenophobia[c]

Sources: (a) *Syracuse Herald-Journal,* May 28, 1969; (b) *Gananda, Program
Plan A,* p. 48; (c) *Riverton Application for Guarantee Assistance,* November 30,
1970, pp. 31–32.

attitudes toward the proposals, and concerns, are shown in Table
6.2.

Each example indicated that the developer's leadership, the
characteristics of the developer's organization, and the method of
presenting the proposal to the public influenced the emergence
of controversy. We can ask ourselves whether there are still other
issues which become apparent as strong influences on the course
of events during the proposal phase. This question must be answered within certain limits. It will be recalled that the focus of
the case studies was on the proposal phase of the project, that is,
in the presentation of the project to the community. Conflict
emerges at this point to reach culmination in a community vote,
or votes, by elected officials. The nature of the process extends
the period of potential conflict from a single vote or several votes
by elected officials to a series of approvals required as development continues over time—and as the developer and community
become "partners." Disruption of this relationship can nega-

tively affect the future of the project just as much as conflict in the proposal phase of the project.

An additional factor in the urban-development process involves the actions by bureaucratic agencies of government during the planning phase(s) of all types of projects. These include local, regional, federal, and state agencies. As a result of the environmental protection legislation of the early 1970's, regional agencies were created, and their existence provides an additional potential conflict party. Two other central issues should be added to this list: community leadership; and government bureaucracies.

Local Community Leadership. Local community leadership in urban development was conceived of earlier as being represented by the actions of elected officials. Furthermore, it was considered that elected officials function as parties in the conflict relationship in response to actions by the developer. This simple model is appropriate for urban development involved in a singularly controversial issue, such as zoning for a single-use proposal or a public facility. However, as projects become more comprehensive, such as those involving a variety of land uses or a staged process of development, the stakes for members of the existing community become higher. The third party seeks expression of its dissatisfaction over an aggrieved feeling that elected leaders are not adequately concerned over the stakes which are being affected.[20] Because of the nature of a comprehensive project, the developer must return to the elected leaders for additional approval of phase proposals. At each occurrence the developer exposes himself to third parties seeking opportunities for satisfaction of grievances.

We have seen that third parties develop as exposure creates issues of controversy. In Henrietta and Wayne County antagonistic third parties rejected the decisions of elected leaders in later stages of project development. What becomes evident is that the new-community projects (and other comprehensive forms of urban development which evolve into partnership approaches with local government over a period of time) suggest the inclu-

20. The alienated individual and political behavior was investigated by Robert L. Crain, Elihu Katz, and Donald B. Rosenthal in *The Politics of Community Conflict* (New York: Bobbs-Merrill, 1969). See also, William Kornhauser, *The Politics of Mass Society* (New York: The Free Press, 1959).

sion of characteristics of community leaders into a theoretical framework. The results of a vote or votes by elected officials are inadequate for understanding community leadership as a central issue. This must be expanded to examine the interaction of community leaders with other factors previously described.

Bureaucratic Influence. One of our basic premises—that local leadership represents the community in the conflict relationship in the form of one or several votes—has been disrupted by the introduction of additional parties into the process. As we saw in the new-community proposals, the effect of the clearinghouse review by regional authorities was to create conflict in Riverton and Gananda. Criticism by the state legislature resulted in the creation of new legislation which restrained UDC from certain actions at Lysander.

Two other investigations on local decision-making, one in New York City and one on suburban areas, also document that a portion of local leadership responsibilities has been transferred from elected officials and the community elite to bureaucracies of technical and administrative staff. Wallace S. Sayre and Herbert Kaufman considered bureaucrats in New York City's government as important participants in city politics.[21] The regulatory, enforcement, and service functions of government performed by these officials affect public services and, in turn, are instrumental in relations with the general public. In his study of *Suburbia,* Robert C. Wood investigated relationships of elected officials and the community. He found that in suburban and other urbanizing areas the roles of elected officials did not follow stereotyped models of political institutions. Instead, he found that the influence of nonpartisanship attitudes in suburban and rural areas suggested that it is not the citizen but the local bureaucrat who is the most influential. What Wood discovered was that in municipalities where party politics exist, even if predominately one-party politics, there are professional politicians who make it their business to know developments and who act in expert capacity. However, where nonpartisanship holds sway, function by function, more and more public activities are called administrative and professional and placed in the hands of specialists in technical matters.

21. Wallace S. Sayre and Herbert Kaufman, *Governing New York City* (New York: Russell Sage Foundation, 1960), Part III.

Ultimately, local debate centers on three issues: honesty, the tax bill, and land development. This was the case in the three new-community proposals. Technical matters in Lysander were not raised as a controversial issue. The Homeowners' Association chose to develop a strategy based on the conceptual content of the plan for the project and the procedural format under UDC powers. Riverton Properties argued with the bureaucracies reviewing the A-95 material and with HUD's New Communities Office about the projected population of Riverton. At Gananda, acceptance of the plan by the residents of Walworth and Macedon did not prevent the planners in adjacent Monroe County from generating conflict over the proposal. Eventually, the ongoing controversies over each project seemed to be divided between bureaucratic review of technical matters outside of local government and conflict with local elected officials and other community leaders over the integrity of the developer and the fiscal impact of the project on the community.

Wood concluded that, more and more frequently, the reality of control seems to rest on the shoulders of relatively few, either elected officials or informal leaders, who stand between a bureaucracy and the nonpartisan public. This conclusion supports observations on the importance of the issue of local leadership and introduces another level of control into the conflict relationship: the supportive, or nonsupportive, actions of local bureaucratic officials.

Two propositions can be added to those described earlier (see Chapter 1, pages 35–36):

19. Where politics is nonpartisan, bureaucratic influence on technical decisions is an important factor in the conflict relationship.
20. In nonpartisan areas the critical issues of fiscal matters and land development are decided by elected officials or informal leaders.

Epilogue

From program inception in 1968 through the summer of 1975 the HUD new-communities program and the three upstate New York projects advanced from concept into construction.

We can consider several things by reviewing the evolution of Radisson, Riverton, and Gananda during this period. How have they fared in comparison to original plans? How have the conditions we concluded as influencing development affected the projects? And, because of the unique nature of new communities as long-term projects what are the effects of local leaders, bureaucratic influence, and state and national interests on the projects.

The 1975 position of the two privately supported projects, Riverton and Gananda, might be best described by the headlines in a Rochester newspaper that reported weeds reigning where planners dreamed of lawns: "Seeds of Hope Yield Weeds, symbolic of Gananda plight." By January, 1974, seventeen of the HUD-designated new communities, including Radisson, Riverton, and Gananda, were plagued by inability to meet the sales and cash-flow projections that would have enabled them to pay the interest charges on bonds they sold. As HUD-guaranteed bond interest came due in late 1973 and early 1974, the effects of the national economic recession on construction impacted on new communities. Early cash-flow projections were thrown off as development costs and interest rates soared and at the same time cash from sales of land and buildings failed to materialize.

The purpose of the federal new-community-program financial support was to provide guarantees of loans for purchase and development of land and to assist in the planning and installation of utilities, roads, and other public facilities. Funds a developer received from the federally guaranteed obligations could not be used to build residential, commercial, and industrial structures. Public and private developers became involved with the federal program with a view to obtaining supplementary grants for public services, gaining priority access to subsidies for housing and, it was hoped, gaining leverage for better financing rates due to the government guarantees. The first full year of program funding in 1972 saw no congressional appropriation, and a HUD appropriation was impounded by the U.S. Office of Management and Budget. After June, 1973, HUD ended the supplemental grant program. The impounding of housing subsidy funds in 1973 further exacerbated the developers' dilemmas.

By late 1974, Riverton and Gananda representatives were negotiating with HUD officials for refinancing of their projects. Riverton management was successful in obtaining additional HUD guarantees for loans; Gananda was not. Part of the financial problem in the developments was due to the impoundment of funds for community facilities and housing by the Nixon administration in 1973. These funds were necessary to provide the much-needed capital for improving the land and providing amenities. For example, the 40 percent portion of housing designated for low-income families could not go ahead without federal subsidy. Sewer and lighting systems to be aided by programs identified for the priority of new communities were not installed because of the slowdown in funding.

The combination of soaring development costs, the unavailability of financial aid from federal sources, and the national economic recession left the three projects far behind original schedules. Radisson was probably the most viable of the three projects by the summer of 1975. Extensive site work was installed which gave the project an air of progress. Roads with design relationship sensitive to the terrain were completed, with grass shoulders, lighting, and street signs in place; utilities for the areas that were scheduled for residential construction were completed in anticipation of improved market conditions. Single-family homes and town houses of good architectural design were under construction with a target of 200 for the fall of 1975. The first building sites were in heavily wooded areas which are attractive for marketing.

Several other buildings have been completed and are in use on the site. A community center with outdoor pool and recreation space is fed by a completed network of pedestrian and bicycle paths. A temporary neighborhood health center was in operation until destroyed by fire. Construction has started on a replacement permanent building.

The Urban Development Corporation, although virtually terminated in 1973 due to its fiscal situation, has sustained the Radisson project. This was accomplished in part because its corporate structure was separate from that of the parent corporation, and in part because of the administrative actions of the State of New York in support of the project. The most telling evidence of the state's support was the assistance given in securing the location of a major industry for Radisson. Schlitz Brewing Company has constructed a brewery and can factory which will cost over $50 million for the first stage of construction. Hundreds of construction jobs have been created, and over a thousand permanent jobs will be available when the plant is in full operation. The brewery project gives the site an air of intense activity, and the visitor has an overall impression that Radisson is a going development. Unfortunately, this is not the case for Gananda or Riverton.

By the summer of 1975 Riverton Properties had made tangible progress on its site. Approximately 800 people were living on the site in a mix of detached single-family homes, townhouses, and multifamily units. Roads and paths were in place, a lake built, and community facilities with outdoor pool and tennis courts were in use. An attractive nine-hole golf course was open to the satisfied critical eyes of area golfers. The developed area was a modest portion of the total and, except for the golf course, was a treeless and grassless site. Unlike the verdant areas of Radisson, the housing area of Riverton offered little visual appeal seven years after the project was first proposed. An attempt to mix building types and architectural styles was unsuccessful, and the architectural design of the housing was unattractive.

Business interests in Riverton existed in a small commercial building, in the building housing the Riverton Properties office, and in a community center building. About forty to fifty people were employed on the site other than in construction, and a dozen or so of these were the development company's employees. The developers were frustrated in attracting industry to improve cash flow because of the difficult vehicle access to the site and the lack of extension of utilities to the site.

The Riverton project reached a financial crisis in mid-1973. Project staff was drastically cut and building on the site virtually stopped by late 1974 when the company announced imminent bankruptcy. After lengthy negotiations with HUD a refinancing agreement was reached for an arrangement that totaled $6.1 million in equity, bonds, and credit. The Riverton agreement includes HUD's approval for the sale of another $4 million of HUD-guaranteed bonds, in addition to the $12 million issued in May, 1972. Riverton shareholders agreed to put up $1 million in equity, and private banks agreed to a new $1.1 million credit package. Riverton shareholders also agreed to purchase some of the project's land if revenue falls below the latest three-year projections, and agreed to maintain a minimum cash balance. HUD agreed to stretch out the life of the project for another two years beyond 1988 and to reduce the required percentage of low and moderate-income housing units from 40 to 25 percent. These arrangements appeared to offer a measure of fiscal stability.

Rochester's other federally guaranteed new community, Gananda, has not fared as well as Riverton. By the summer of 1975 the Gananda Development Corporation was in arrears on interest payments and had ceased all building activities on the site. Staff had been reduced to a minimal "caretaker" operation. The only completed evidence of the project was a community center-school building, an information center, and some site work. Gananda's problems began to emerge in ways similar to Riverton in 1973. However, the overambitious scope of Gananda seems to have accelerated its difficulties as cash flow failed to meet income demands for interest repayment and fresh construction capital. Starting in early 1974 the project received monthly setbacks. A complete management turnover occurred; federal support for a 450-acre park was cut, and the park was reduced to 240 acres; union troubles followed when Gananda created its own construction company to replace contractors already on site; a county plan to provide the project with water was not endorsed; and county support for a four-lane access parkway was withdrawn. By mid-1974 development schedules and plans for subsidized housing were drastically redrawn to half the original estimates. Local government and former property owners became alarmed in late 1974 when Gananda actively sought to renegotiate terms of land sales. By the summer of 1975 the Corporation's activity consisted of attempts to refinance and efforts to maintain a public awareness of the project.

Both private new-community projects suffered from lack of cash flow and reserves which were available to the publicly supported Radisson. It becomes apparent that the developers' difficulties were due in part to issues outside of their control and beyond those of local communities. Distress about the lack of progress and concern for the national investment in new communities resulted in the Comptroller General of the United States preparing a Report to Congress on the subject: *Getting the New Communities Program Started: Progress and Problems.*[22] The focus of

22. Comptroller General of the United States Report to Congress, *Getting the New Communities Started: Progress and Problems* (Washington, D.C., Nov., 1974).

198 | THE BUILDING OF CITIES

the report was on inaccuracies in market feasibility and the financial feasibility of original project designs. Many of the projects with HUD guarantees suffered from their management team's inexperience in large-scale developments.

Interviews with participants in the projects and reviews of the newspaper reporting during the early years of development indicate that other factors may have affected progress in addition to lack of federal financial support. Certainly Radisson won local support when the huge industrial development on the site was announced. Further positive interest occurred when another large brewery project was announced for an adjacent town. Riverton and Gananda seem to have raised suspicions among local leaders and elected officials about credibility when announced schedules failed to be met. And, in some cases, relations with officials who were depended upon for cooperation in processing grant applications were strained because of the personality and actions of the developers' staff.

The worst possible result occurred for Riverton and Gananda: the local communities distrusted the developers. Regardless of how carefully explanations were made, the developers could not convince the communities that the problems were not a devious real estate scheme, but were instead due to federal actions and national economic changes. Radisson, Riverton, and Gananda's early disassociation from identification with the existing community alienated local residents, and antagonisms were revived when the developer tried to overcome this changing marketing strategy to appease local feelings. Town board members in all three communities expressed distaste for the developers' contempt for local values when their opinions were originally ignored.

When financial strain for the private developers caused the need for greater dependency on local governments and elected officials, early grievances were brought up and caused project delays above and beyond federal actions. Antagonisms of personalities and unsatisfactory relations were aggravated as the posture of the developers had to be modified. In this kind of environment local officials adopted a more conservative stance toward cooperating with the developers. Continuing media discussions of the Rochester projects have emphasized management instability and fiscal problems. This type of exposure is not conducive to maintaining cooperation from elected leaders or appointed officials.

While project progress was hampered by personal interaction and by the local self-interests that were being expressed, other principled arguments emerged. Gananda was affected by this, as Monroe County officials continued to criticize the project as being contradictory to rational metropolitan development. As a result, planners in county and regional agencies have given the project weak support. Attitudes such as these contributed to Gananda's problems.

The unusual conditions of a presidential impoundment of federal funds and a national construction recession placed the three new communities in a state of limbo early in their development. Because progress was slow, it has been possible to return to each community and review early controversies with a matured eye. The private developers have not been able to maintain their credibility as changing fiscal conditions affected project progress. A town supervisor in a rural community who has been barely convinced of a project's merits views a developer's accusations of Washington's perfidy with doubt. It appears that the credibility of the developer is a fragile thing, and any project delays are harmful. Also, the personalities of the developers are critical for project success.

In conclusion, we should ask: What are the avenues for future study? One of our goals was to understand the interactions of parties and organizations which lead either to acceptance or to rejection of a proposal for change. Attention has been drawn to this need not only in this study but elsewhere.[23] Additional research is suggested for the following areas.

(1) *The interaction between project leadership, community elite, and bureaucratic officials.* We know that each of these groups influenced the progress of the project in its planning phase, but we do not know how each affected the other. For example, it would assist our understanding to know the effect of differing positions by community elite and bureaucratic officials to a proposal.

23. The report of the Land Use Subcommittee of the Advisory Committee to the Department of Housing and Urban Development, *Urban Growth and Land Development* (Washington, D.C., 1972), p. 43, describes this as "development of a firmer understanding of the participants in the land conversion process and the effects of their participation."

(2) *The influence of the type of project on the position taken by the community elite or bureaucratic officials.* We have studied one type of project in the three illustrations: new communities. Research that shows how different types of projects (redevelopment, highway location, public-utility expansion) affect the community elite and bureaucratic officials' attitudes toward areas of concern would contribute to an understanding, generally, of conflict over urban development.

(3) *The effect of the community setting on the emergence of controversy.* The general locale of the three new-community case studies was in rural or suburban areas. The usefulness of the theoretical framework can be evaluated by examining the emergence of controversy over urban development in urban areas.

(4) *Testing of the twenty propositions on a broader sample of case studies.* Recalling our earlier description of methodology, the central issues and propositions were "working hypotheses" to help interpret certain data and guide investigation. The mere fact that they had to be formulated helped to focus attention on areas of study, as well as provide a frame of reference for examining relationships between parties, and between parties and their environment. We have concluded in this chapter that investigation into additional issues would further the understanding of the subject. Testing of the stated propositions should be helpful.[24]

These suggested areas of research would increase the extent of knowledge about community conflict that occurs when urban development programs are in progress. There is a subtle and underlying theme in this subject. When the goals of a developer are congruent with those of a community, there is little disagreement. As goals diverge there is an increased tendency for conflict to emerge. Study of several new-community proposals illustrates this pattern: elected officials who interpret an urban-develop-

24. We agree with other investigators of community problems that knowledge possessed by the author prior to the study and not formulated into hypotheses also guided the research. It must be admitted that it was necessary on occasion to remind ourselves that we had hypotheses to refer to. Herbert Gans, *The Urban Villagers* (New York: The Free Press, 1962), and Arthur Vidich and Joseph Bensman, *Small Town in Mass Society* (Princeton: Princeton University Press, 1958), added appendixes to their works to describe similar conclusions. See also Floyd Hunter's conclusions on "Working Hypotheses," in *Community Organization: Action and Inaction* (Chapel Hill: University of North Carolina Press, 1956), pp. 226–240.

ment proposal as beneficial to a community will tend to approve the necessary modifications to existing regulations and ordinances. Before this action is taken, only a few voices may have been raised in opposition, either through citizens' committees or Letters to the Editor in the local media. As the need for public action draws near, public sentiment begins to build up against a proposal. The difference between a community's goals and those of the developer are stressed for their divisive effect. The developer's task becomes one of convincing the community elite and the local bureaucracy of the similarity of goals between the community and the planning proposal. As the development period extends over time, then the developer must not only gain local acceptance, but must maintain this confidence for the duration of the project.

Expansion of knowledge on this subject and the application of findings to urban development proposals can assist in reducing community conflict. This task should certainly be of benefit to developers engaged in projects with a potential for controversy. An awareness of the factors we have discussed can aid the elected local leaders and community elite in accepting the challenge of improving the quality of the physical environment through proposals for development and redevelopment. Bureaucratic officials, the architects, engineers and planners, and the legal professionals who are involved in urban development are challenged to apply these findings for the benefit of their community and all of its members. Most importantly, people who formulate policy and make decisions about urban development must be made aware of the factors we have discussed and be prepared to apply them to minimize community conflict.

Appendix | Macedon-Walworth New Community District Zoning Ordinance

SECTION 1. Statement of Intent and Objectives

It is the intent of this Ordinance to establish a special planned unit development district within the Town of Macedon, and a special planned unit development district within the town of Walworth to be known as The Macedon-Walworth New Community District, which district shall consist of approximately 10,500 contiguous acres of land. Said district shall hereinafter be referred to as "New Community District" (NCD).

In order that there be uniform administration and development of the property located within the NCD, the Town of Macedon and the Town of Walworth hereby declare their intent to cooperate in the administration, planning and approval procedures and in the services and government covering the area located within the NCD.

In order to carry out the intent of this section the NCD shall promote the following objectives:

a. Maximum choice in the types of environment, occupancy, tenure, (e.g., cooperatives, individual ownership, condominiums, leasing), types of housing, lot sizes and community facilities available to Town residents at all economic levels;

b. More usable open space and recreation areas;

c. More convenience in location of accessory commercial and service areas;

d. Development patterns which preserve trees, outstanding natural topography and geologic features and prevent soil erosion;

e. Creative use of land and related physical developments which allow an orderly transition of land from rural to urban uses;

f. Efficient use of land resulting in smaller networks of utilities and streets and thereby lower housing costs;

g. Development patterns in harmony with the objectives of the individual Towns;

h. A more desirable environment than would be possible through ordinary zoning procedures.

This section specifically encourages innovation in residential development so that the growing demands for housing at all economic levels may be met by greater variety in type, design and siting of dwellings and by the conservation and more efficient use of land in such developments. This article recognizes that while the standard zoning function (use and bulk) and the subdivision (platting and design) are appropriate for the regulation of land in areas or neighborhoods that are already substantially developed, these controls may represent a type of preregulation, regulatory rigidity and uniformity which may be inimical to the technique of land development to be promoted in the new community district.

SECTION 2. General Requirements

A. Location of NCD

The NCD is hereby adopted for 10,500 acres of land located partly within the Town of Macedon and partly within the Town of Walworth as shown on the map adopted with this Ordinance. Said map may be revised by a showing that the developer, or any successor thereto, has obtained control of additional adjacent land and that the inclusion of such land within the NCD will be to the benefit of the new planned community and the Town wherein the land is located. Prior to the revision of said map the recommendation for inclusion of additional land shall be submitted to the Joint Preliminary Review Board, as established by this Ordinance. Approval for such inclusion of additional land shall be by the Town Board governing the area within which such additional land is located, pursuant to the provisions of the Town Law of the State of New York.

B. Permitted Uses in Macedon-Walworth New Community District

(1) Dwelling units, detached, semi-detached, attached, clustered, or a combination thereof, whether single family, multiplex, low or high rise apartments.

(2) Commercial, service and other non-residential uses.

(3) Public and private institutional and recreational facilities.

(4) Office, research and manufacturing uses.

C. Roads and Utilities

The developer shall provide all necessary water and sewer facilities, storm drainage, highway access, paved service streets, parking and loading facilities, off street lighting, sidewalks and curbs as shall be required by the appropriate town, except as may otherwise be provided through State, County or Federal programs.

D. Common Property

Community property in the NCD shall be a parcel or parcels of land, together with the improvements thereon, the use and enjoyment of which are shared by the residents and/or employees of the community. When common property exists, the ownership of such common property may be either public, community, private or any combination thereof. When common property exists arrangements satisfactory to the Joint Preliminary Review Board and the appropriate town boards must be made for the improvement, operation and maintenance of such common property and facilities, including private streets, drives, service and parking areas and recreational and open space areas. The Joint Preliminary Review Board and the individual town board shall retain the right to review and approve the articles of incorporation and character of any association which will own or manage any common property within the NCD, and to require whatever conditions it deems necessary to insure that the intent and purpose of this Ordinance is carried out.

E. Residential Density

The land use density for the total acreage covered by this NCD shall not exceed four (4) dwelling units per acre.

SECTION 3. Required Planning Board Review

Site development plans approved by the Planning Board of the town wherein the property is located shall be required for all proposed developments. Where an approved site development plan is proposed to be amended, such amendment shall also be subject to the approval of the appropriate town planning board.

On each original or amended site development plan the town planning board shall certify whether or not the said plan meets all applicable requirements of this Ordinance.

No building permit or certificate of occupancy may be issued by the building inspector nor may any division of property be made except in accordance with an approved site development plan, or amendment of any such plan.

SECTION 4. Review Standards

In acting on site development plans, the appropriate planning board shall take into consideration the objectives, guidelines and conditions of this Ordinance, and shall be further guided by the following standards which, shall not, however, be considered firm requirements, and which may be varied by the board.

A. Residential Standards

(1) Areas proposed in the form of single family detached houses shall not exceed the density set forth in Section 2 D.

(2) To the extent feasible, at least 30 percent of the total number of dwellings within this NCD should be in single family detached structures.

(3) The densities for low rise residential areas shall not exceed 14 dwelling units per acre.

(4) Building height, size and design shall be appropriate to the location within the NCD where proposed, and shall further be appropriate to the overall development plan of the NCD and the particular development plan of the individual town wherein the property is located.

(5) There shall be off street parking facilities which shall be adequate for the particular development and determined by the appropriate town planning board wherein the property is located. In no case shall campers, boats and other recreational vehicles be stored in other than screened or enclosed structures.

(6) Landscaped open spaces or open areas left in their natural state should be provided at a ratio of not less than 600 square feet of open space for every dwelling unit. The appropriate town planning board may require as much as 25% of this required acreage to be provided in the form of suitable play areas.

(7) All multi-family uses must provide adequate landscaping to the satisfaction of the appropriate town planning board wherein the property is located.

(8) A buffer strip of adequate width should be provided where appropriate, between residential and non-residential areas and between residential areas and state and county roads. Said buffer strip may be created by utilizing suitably landscaped green areas, by design, configuration and location of particular buildings, or by any other method meeting the approval of the appropriate town planning board. No parking shall be permitted in a buffer area.

(9) In order to provide the necessary full range of housing for all residents who may wish to be employed within the new community, it is hereby provided that up to 15% of the total number of housing units may make such payments in lieu of taxes as shall be required to comply with state and federal subsidy programs which require a tax adjustment. It shall be deemed most in keeping with this Ordinance to have such subsidized housing units scattered throughout the residential areas and projects and not concentrated in separate geographical locations. The appropriate town planning board is hereby delegated the authority by the Town of Macedon and the Town of Walworth to approve the location of such units, their compliance with the established state and federal housing subsidy programs, and the appropriate amounts of payments in lieu of taxes as necessary under such established state and federal programs, all in compliance with Article XI of the New York State Private Housing Finance Law, and such other sections of New York Law as shall be applicable.

B. Commercial Standards

(1) Except for the regional commercial center located within the NCD, commercial uses should be generally scaled to serve the residents of the NCD. A maximum of one-half acre of land for every 100 dwelling units should be used for commercial service purposes.

(2) Parking areas serving commercial uses shall be provided at a minimum ratio of one square foot of parking space for every one (1) square foot of retail area.

C. Office, Research and Manufacturing Standards

(1) The amount of land devoted to office, research and manufacturing uses shall be appropriate to the overall development of the NCD.

(2) Office and Research use shall be subject to controls as deemed appropriate by the governing body of the Town wherein the property is located.

(3) The industrial uses are to be located within the Towns of Macedon and Walworth in approximate proportion to the respective acreage as shown on the map of the NCD adopted with this Ordinance, and as such map shall be amended from time to time.

D. Site and Structure Standards

(1) Where feasible, natural features such as streams, rocks, outcrops, topsoil, trees and shrubs shall be preserved and incorporated in the landscaping of the development.

(2) Where adequate surface drainage is not possible by grading alone,

a supplementary drainage system approved by the appropriate town shall be required.

(3) To improve the quality of the environment and to reduce inconvenience during bad weather, the underground installation of electrical and telephone equipment shall be required where feasible.

(4) Lot size and dimensions, structure heights and locations thereon, may be freely disposed and arranged in conformity with the overall density standards set forth herein. Minimum lot size or frontage and, except for office, research and manufacturing uses, maximum percentage of lot coverages, are not specified herein. In reviewing any particular site plan for the whole or any part of property falling within this NCD the board shall be guided by the appropriate standards of good planning practices, to the end that the resulting development shall be compatible with the surroundings of the area and assure the stability of the uses proposed to be developed on the site.

(5) The right of way and pavement widths for internal roads serving multi-family dwellings, commercial and office, research and manufacturing developments shall be determined from sound planning and engineering standards to conform with the estimated needs of the proposed full development and the traffic to be generated thereby. The pavement of said roads shall not be less than 24 feet wide, excluding parking lanes, and shall be adequate and sufficient in size, location and design to accommodate the maximum traffic, parking and loading needs and the access of fire fighting equipment and police emergency vehicles. Dedicated streets shall be in conformance with the standards established by the appropriate town.

SECTION 5. Application Procedures

A. General Requirements

The Planning Board shall require the applicant to furnish such preliminary drawings and specifications as required for normal site development plan approval, including the following:

(1) An area map showing applicants' entire holdings, said portion of the applicants' property under consideration, and all properties, subdivisions, streets and easements within 500 feet of that parcel of property. An applicant shall also show whether its holdings are by lease, option, deed or otherwise.

(2) A topographic map showing contour intervals of not more than 5 feet of elevation.

(3) A plan map showing the location of the various uses, the general pattern of the interior road systems, the location and treatment of

all open space areas (including parks and playgrounds) and the location of all existing and proposed site improvements, including water, sewer and storm drainage systems. In addition, data on the number of dwelling units by type and the approximate acreages for all uses shall be included on the plan, if available.

(4) Any other material deemed necessary to determine the applicability of the development with special reference to:

(i) the proposed developments, land use and circulation patterns and their relationship to natural features;

(ii) the proposed developments relating to the existing structures and uses in adjacent areas.

B. Approval of Plans

The Town Planning Board is hereby delegated the authority to give final approval to site development or plot plans, pursuant to the provisions of the Town Law of the State of New York.

C. References to Joint Preliminary Review Board

All site plans shall be submitted to the Joint Preliminary Review Board for their review and recommendations prior to submission to the appropriate town planning board.

SECTION 6. Construction Time Limitations

If, after the passage of 24 months from the date of approval of this New Community District, construction has not substantially commenced, the approval given under the terms of this Ordinance shall be revoked and the land shall then be returned to the zoning classification which it held prior to any action consummated pursuant to the provisions of this ordinance.

SECTION 7. Staging

It is anticipated that the developer will stage development within this NCD and said developer may submit in detail those stages he wishes to develop for site plan approval in accordance with a staging plan. Such plan must be submitted and approved for each stage of development in accordance with the procedures established within this ordinance.

The developers shall present annually to each town planning board a master plan showing existing developments, and the projected development for the succeeding three years, together with an analysis of the long term projected conformance with land use ratios and the other requirements of this ordinance.

At no time in the development of this NCD shall the ratio of non-residential to residential development be unnecessarily excessive.

SECTION 8. Petition for Revision of Approval Plan

At any time following approval of site plans, including the issuance of permits for any part thereof, the applicant may petition for review in detail the previously approved plan, stating his reasons therefor. Such reason may be based upon such considerations as, but shall not be limited to, changing social or economic conditions, suggested improvement to layout or design features, or unforeseen difficulties or advantages such as site conditions, state or federal projects, or statutory changes, which may mutually affect the interest of the applicant and the town wherein the property is located. The planning board of the town wherein the property is located upon finding that such petition and reasons are reasonable and valid and provided that such revisions do not after the concept of the plan as previously approved, and after receiving the recommendations of the Joint Preliminary Review Board, may reconsider the design of all or a portion of the site plan.

SECTION 9. Improvements or Performance Guarantees

As a condition of final approval of site plans the Planning Board may require the applicant to install all site improvements or to post adequate performance guarantees to insure the installation of said improvements in an amount sufficient to cover the cost of all such improvements. Said performance guarantee may be in the form of a performance bond which shall be issued by a bonding surety company approved by the town, or certified check, which should include an agreed upon date for the completion of such improvements and should be for a period of time determined by the planning board. The amount of the performance guarantee may be reduced by the planning board when portions of the required improvements have been completed. If no such bond or performance guarantee is posted, the approval or application shall be a nullity.

SECTION 10. Building Requirements Within New Community District

It is the purpose of this article to provide for housing at all economic levels using a wide variety of type, design and siting in a more effective use of land and land spaces. It is also expected that new and effective construction methods will lower the cost of construction and make housing available to residents of this NCD at a more reasonable cost. It is understood that some traditional building codes are not in keeping with the above purposes of this article. Therefore, it is hereby provided that those sections of the New York State Statutes as apply to fire, health and safety as well as electrical, plumbing, heating, ventilating and air conditioning and other construction requirements shall be the sole governing codes for construction within the NCD. All construction of all buildings, structures and facilities must be in compliance with the appropriate governing requirements as set forth in the New York State Statutes. The appropriate New York State Statutes shall likewise be the sole governing requirements for all sewer, water, gas, electrical and communications installations and transmission facilities, and all such installation and facilities must be in compliance with the appropriate sections of the New York State Statutes.

SECTION 11. Joint Preliminary Review Board

A. Purpose and Intent

Because of the size of the tract of land covered by this ordinance, and the long range development requirements for such a large tract, and because it is desirable that the Town of Macedon and the Town of Walworth promote creativity and flexibility within the purpose and intent provision of this ordinance, as well as to maintain the high standards that are required for the welfare of the residents of the new community, the Town of Macedon and the Town of Walworth hereby agree to cooperate with each other and the developers to provide for expeditious and consistent approvals and administration in accordance with this ordinance.

B. Membership

There is hereby established by the Town of Macedon and the Town of Walworth, a Joint Preliminary Review Board to review and/or approve all necessary site plans and permits within the NCD. Whereby New York State law approvals are required by a specific town board or planning board the Joint Preliminary Review Board will make the necessary recommendations to such board or boards.

The Joint Preliminary Review Board shall consist of eight members, two members each to be chosen by and represent the planning boards of the Town of Macedon and the planning board of the Town of Walworth, one member to be chosen by the Wayne County Planning Board, and the remaining members to be chosen by and to represent the developers. Such representatives shall serve at the pleasure of the respective board or the developers they represent. Each board making a designation or appointment to said Joint Preliminary Review Board may appoint an alternate representative, who shall be authorized and permitted to represent the Board in the absence of the official appointee. The Planning Board, or its representatives on the review board, may request appropriate consultants employed by the Planning Board or appropriate employees of the Town to attend any meetings of said preliminary review board.

C. Functions

The Joint Preliminary Review Board shall discuss and review development proposals, and make recommendations thereon, prior to submission to the appropriate planning board. In addition, all proposed zoning changes, zoning variances and non-residential developments in the town located within 800 yards of this NCD shall be submitted to said board for their review and recommendations.

Actions of the Joint Preliminary Review Board shall in no way bind the Planning Board, Town Board, Board of Appeals or Building Inspector or other appropriate Town officials or board, nor shall failure of the Joint Preliminary Review Board to act in a reasonable period of time (as determined by the appropriate Town official or board) restrict the action of the Planning Board, Town Board, Board of Appeals or other appropriate Town official or board.

SECTION 12. Non-Conforming Uses

(1) Any building or land located within the NCD, and lawfully occupied by a use on the date of the first publication of the public hearing notice for the enactment of this Ordinance, or amendment thereto, which does not conform after the passing of this Ordinance, or amendment thereto, to the permitted uses or regulations of the NCD shall be deemed a nonconforming use.

(2) Such use deemed non-conforming may be continued, but if said non-conforming use or occupancy be discontinued for a period of more than twelve months, it shall be deemed abandoned, and any subsequent use or occupancy of the land or structure shall be in conformance with the provisions of the NCD.

(3) A use deemed non-conforming may be changed to a use permitted in the NCD provided the change is approved by the Joint Preliminary Review Board. Once a non-conforming use has been changed to an approved conforming use said building or land shall not be permitted to revert to a non-conforming use.

(4) A use deemed non-conforming shall not be enlarged, extended or intensified, nor shall any structural alteration be made to any building in which said use is conducted, except as may be specifically permitted by the Joint Preliminary Review Board.

SECTION 13. Governing Provisions

In order to promote innovative planning, development and to foster creative use of the property located therein, the NCD shall be governed by and subject only to the provisions set forth in this Ordinance and the provisions set forth in the Zoning Ordinance of the Town of Macedon and the Town of Walworth regulating zoning districts, and establishing minimum requirements and use restrictions shall not be applicable within this district, except as may have been specifically provided herein and as may be required by the Joint Preliminary Review Board upon their review of an application, or plan, for a use of the whole or any part of the property located within this district.

Index

Sayre, Wallace S., 192
Samuels, Howard, 139-140
Schiener, Jane, 86
Schneider, James B., 86
Searles, John, 96
Simon, Robert E., 23, 135, 139-142, 149,
    156, 159, 162-170, 175, 188
Smith, Chester, 79, 88-93, 97-98
Snyder, Richard, 188
Stafford, Richard, 86
Stainton, John, 78, 81, 147-168
Syracuse, N.Y., 22, 24, 69, 72
Syracuse Herald Journal, 82
Syracuse University Research Corpora-
    tion (SURC):
    at Lysander, 79, 83-84, 94
    at Gananda, 125

Terry, John, 95
Thompson, Walter P., 86

Uptegrove, William, 114
Urban land development

participants, 59-66
process, 48-51
social values, 44-47
Urbanization, 39-67
    impact, 44
    patterns, 41
    suburbanization, 42-44, 175

Vidich, Arthur, 34

Walworth, town of, 104-105, 110, 112,
    117, 123
Wayne County, 103, 104, 118
    planning board, 121
Weiss, Shirley, 50, 54-55
Wilson, James W., 29
Wilson, Jerome, 129
Wood, Robert C., *Suburbia*, 43, 192-193

Zoning, 182-184, 203-213; *see also*
    Land-use controls

www.ingramcontent.com/pod-product-compliance
Lightning Source LLC
Chambersburg PA
CBHW031131270326
41929CB00011B/1588